ON MY KNEES

Preparing to Enter the Throne Room

Terri Edwards

ISBN 979-8-88616-634-7 (paperback)
ISBN 979-8-88616-635-4 (digital)

Christian Faith Publishing
832 Park Avenue
Meadville, PA 16335
www.christianfaithpublishing.com

Printed in the United States of America

CONTENTS

PREFACE

Commit to the LORD whatever you do
and your plans will succeed.

—Proverbs 16:3 (NIV)

It was a beautiful Wednesday morning in May, and my husband and I were busy trying to get our cottage ready to rent for the very first time. I was busy painting the side porch, and as I was finishing up with the last step, a thought came to mind to write a prayer book. As I started to process that thought, I remember saying, "Lord, you know how I hate to write! It takes me forever to just reply to a text or e-mail, let alone write a book. Lord, I'm willing to commit, but I need you to help me write it." Then he reminded me that I had already been writing daily prayers for my youngest son to pray. God had laid that on my heart months ago, as my son was diagnosed with cancer. "Okay," I thought, "maybe a 365-day prayer book."

As I began to pray and ask God about what this prayer book was to include, other thoughts came pouring out. I didn't know if I was supposed to stop praying and grab a pen and paper or just continue to stay on my knees praying. I chose to stay on my knees asking the Lord to help me remember everything he was wanting the prayer book to include.

He reminded me of my own prayer journey and how he has been grooming me for some time, drawing on my experiences with prayer groups and small groups, leading women's ministries, serving at my church as director of pastoral care for women, working with support groups and individual lay counseling sessions. He reminded me of all the things I either faced in my own life or with others I had helped: abortion, alcohol and drug addictions, eating disorders, sexual addictions, anxiety, depression, fear, worry, financial hardships, fertility issues, spiritually mismatched marriages, divorce, single parenting, prodigals, sexual abuse, and suicide. The list is long, but what I have learned from my own experiences and shared with many is that God doesn't waste anything, and he can use it all to bring about good and glory for his name. When I counseled women, my focus was on listening to them and asking questions so I could understand how they felt and then lead them to the only answer and place to go, the throne room. For only God knows how to heal, comfort, or guide them. I was just God's vessel to lead them to him. And, my dear friend, this is what I hope you will allow me to do as you read this book: lead you to his holy throne room, where all are invited.

My Prayer for You

Heavenly Father,

Praise be to the name of God, forever and ever. Lord, I ask your blessings on those that read this book.

I pray that you would speak to their hearts and you would use this book to help lead them to your throne room. And as they enter, to do it with a right spirit that is humbled and willing to submit to you. I ask that they would seek you with all of their heart, all of their soul, and all of their mind. May they go with great expectations of meeting and spending time with you, Lord, and as they do, may they find you.

May their prayer life forever be changed as you draw them closer to you and reveal yourself to them. May you do a mighty work in them, Lord, and may they bring glory to your name.

In Jesus's name I pray.

Amen.

INTRODUCTION

Welcome!

I'm so excited you have chosen to read this book on prayer.

Whether you are praying for yourself, your family, your friends, or others, it is a privilege to be able to approach God knowing that he delights in our seeking him.

On My Knees was written to inspire you to spend time with God, to equip you with an understanding of how to pray with a purpose, and to encourage you with examples of prayers that can help you begin to form your own prayers from Scripture.

On My Knees is designed for you to read, reread, and reference whenever you need a jumpstart on praying. It is a prayer book that you can work through yourself or with a study group.

It is laid out in six parts, each representing an important aspect of prayer. The chapters in each part provide supporting information on that topic. As you read each part you will notice that each one builds on the previous ones, so try to read the book all the way through the first time to better understand the various aspects of prayer.

In part 1, "Preparing for Prayer," we will talk about how to prepare for prayer, which includes examining our hearts, committing to the Lord, and approaching God in a way that is pleasing and honoring to him.

In part 2, "Praying With Purpose," we will discuss how to make the most out of our prayer time by using simple techniques and a bit of structure.

In part 3, "Moving Forward in Prayer," we will dig into the core foundations of being a Christian and the importance of faith, trust, and hope in God so that we may live a life filled with God's peace and strength.

In part 4, "Depending on Prayer," we will address healing and the feelings we face when we deal with various trials in our lives. Each chapter takes a close look at the importance of prayer in handling anxiety, fear, worry, and health issues so that we can have a sound mind and body.

In part 5, "Living in Prayer," we will discuss praying for relationships, children, and finances, including examples of impactful prayers for ourselves or for family and friends that we pray for.

And in part 6, "Practicing to Pray," you will find scriptures that will enhance your prayer life, along with examples of prayers based on those scriptures.

God's communication with us is always consistent with his word. Yet his interactions with his children vary according to the personality of each one. You are about to read the many ways God has interacted with me in my walk with him.

My hope for you as you finish reading *On My Knees* is that you will understand how life-changing and important the power of prayer can be as we are purposeful in our approach to God's holy throne.

PART 1

Preparing for Prayer

CHAPTER 1

It All Begins with the Heart

For where your treasure is, there your heart will be also.

—Matthew 6:21 (NIV)

For many of us, our hearts are filled with life's distractions: work, marriage, kids, home, health, and finances. On top of that, there are so many things going on in the world: political division, social unrest, foreign wars, and inflation. We are not only distracted, but our hearts are heavy. They are full and, in some cases, overflowing with hurt, pain, frustration, and helplessness.

If there was ever a time we needed prayer, it is now! We need to seek our Almighty God! The God that never changes. The God that is the same yesterday, today, and forever. The God that knows all. The God that is omnipotent (all-powerful) and omnipresent (everywhere at the same time). For our God is not only awesome, he is our *hope*! We need to cry out to our Lord, our God. We need to get our hearts right with God and put him at the center of our lives. Our eyes need to be looking to him for wisdom and direction so that we can begin to heal, be restored, and have hope again. For our hope is in the Lord!

We put our hope in the LORD. He is our
help and our shield. In him our hearts rejoice,

> for we trust in his holy name. Let your unfailing
> love surround us, LORD, for our hope is in you
> alone. (Psalm 33:20–22 NLT)

If God were to look at your heart right now, what would he see? Is it a heart that seeks the Lord first and desires for his ways? Or is it more concerned about making money, buying things, or pleasing people? It's okay to want to better ourselves, have nice things, or make friends, but when we start to turn our hearts toward those things and lose sight of God, that's when they become unhealthy for us and displeasing to the Lord.

> But the LORD said to Samuel, "Do not
> consider his [Saul's] appearance or his height, for
> I have rejected him. The LORD does not look
> at the things people look at. People look at the
> outward appearance, but the LORD looks at the
> heart." (1 Samuel 16:7 NIV)

Some of you already have God at the center of your heart and life. Others may need to recommit their lives to God. And some may need to ask Christ into their lives for the first time.

If you would like to recommit to God or ask Christ into your heart for the first time, please pray this prayer:

Heavenly Father,

> I invite you, Lord, into my life. I believe
> that Jesus is God's Son and that he gave his life on
> the cross to pay for my sins. I ask forgiveness for
> my past, present, and future sins and understand
> that I am made clean not by anything I could do
> but what Jesus did for me on the cross. I ask for
> your Holy Spirit to come fill me, and I ask for
> the gift of eternal life. Lord, begin to transform

me into your likeness so that I may bring glory
to your name.

In Jesus's name I pray.
Amen.

Questions

1) What would God see if he was looking at your heart?

2) What kind of changes can you make to ensure God is first in your heart and life?

3) Reread 1 Samuel 16:7. What do you think God meant when he said, "People look at the outward appearance?"

4) In 1 Samuel 16:7, God says, "People look at the outward appearance, but the LORD looks at the heart." What do you think God is looking for in our hearts?

5) God said to Samuel, "I have rejected him." Why do you think God rejected him?

For Reflection

- Put God first in your heart and life.
- Protect your heart by seeking God daily so he remains in your heart.
- Look to God for wisdom and direction.

Prayer for a Right Heart

Heavenly Father,

I ask that you help me to have a right heart before you. Help me not to be distracted by the things of this world but help me to have a heart that seeks you first and a heart that desires your ways. Lord, may I live each day in a way that reflects your image.

In Jesus's name I pray.

Amen.

CHAPTER 2

Committing to the Lord

You will seek me and find me when
you seek me with all your heart.

—Jeremiah 29:13 (NIV)

Do you start your day in prayer? Do you end your day in prayer? Do you spend time in the Word daily? When you have a problem, do you call a friend or do you stop and pray first? Do you take the Lord with you throughout the day, in your car, at your workplace, while you exercise, while cleaning the house, while on vacation, or while you're shopping? Or do you just visit with him on Sunday? Do you believe in God? Do you depend on God?

We ought to open our eyes in the morning with a "Good morning, God" and a word of praise and make that the last activity before we close our eyes at night. King David said, "I will praise the Lord at all times, I will constantly speak his praises" (Psalm 34:1 NLT).

Our Heavenly Father is the one that knows you, that sees the real you, that knows what makes you happy and what makes you sad. He is the one who knows all our dark secrets, and he still wants you to come to him so he can love you, heal you, and comfort you. He also wants to direct your steps and provide wisdom along the way.

Don't worry about your past mistakes. He doesn't ask us to clean ourselves up first. He takes us just as we are, a mess! Don't worry about not being worthy. For our God wants nothing more than for you to come spend time with him, to seek him. His arms are open wide. He's ready and waiting to receive you. All you have to do is go to him, meet him in the throne room, and allow him to work in you and in your life.

Start by committing at least five or ten minutes a day with the Lord. Then find a place that is quiet and has no distractions. Make that your throne room. Bring your Bible or use a phone app to begin reading a chapter a day, or just read one verse. The point is to spend time with God and get to know him. That's why it is so important to read his Word.

Just like any relationship, you need to spend time getting to know the person, understand who they are and what makes them who they are. God has given us his book, the Bible, so we can get to know him. All we have to do is open it up and begin to read so that we can learn about our God and begin to hear and recognize his voice. If you are not familiar with the Bible, begin by reading the Psalm or the Gospel of John.

Quality prayer time involves not only listening to God through his Word but talking to God and sharing your thoughts and concerns with him. It's an opportunity to feel his presence.

> Come near to God and he will come
> near to you. (James 4:8 NIV)

Questions

1) Why do you think it could be important to spend time with God?

____

____

2) Why do you think God doesn't require us to be clean first before coming to him?

____

____

3) What do you think God means in Jeremiah 29:13 when he says, "You will seek me and find me when you seek me with all your heart?"

____

____

4) Why do you think God used the words "all your heart?"

____

____

5) How do you feel when you read James 4:8, "Come near to God and he will come near to you?"

____

____

6) What stands in the way of committing to spend time with God daily? What can you change so you can spend time with God?

____

____

7) If you are ready, take this time to commit to God that you will spend time with him.

____

____

For Reflection

- Commit to spending time with God every day, reading His Word, and praying.
- Just go to God, don't worry about getting yourself clean and perfect. He takes us just as we are.
- As we spend time with God, he begins to transform us into his likeness and reveals himself to us.

Prayer for Committing to God

Heavenly Father,

Your Word says in Jeremiah 29:13, "You will seek me and find me when you seek me with all your heart." Lord, help me to seek you with all my heart so that I can find you and deepen my relationship with you.

Lord, I want to commit five minutes a day to spend time with you. Help me to honor that commitment by going to your throne room, knowing that as I come near to you God, you will come near to me. Remove all that would prevent me from meeting with you. Do not allow me to be distracted, but bless our time together and reveal yourself to me. Help our relationship grow and begin to transform me into your likeness.

In Jesus's name I pray.

Amen.

CHAPTER 3

Approaching the Throne of God

He guides the humble in what is right
and teaches them his way.

—Psalm 25:9 (NIV)

It is so important to remember when we pray that our Father is the God that created the heavens and earth, that he is our Maker, that he is the Alpha and Omega, the beginning and the end.

We need to pray with the right heart, one of reverence and respect. For God is not just anyone. He is the King of kings and the Lord of lords, the God of all gods. He is the Great I Am!

We need to pray for the right reasons. We enter the throne room to spend time with him, to get to know him, and to have a conversation with him. We need to be honest with him and remember that this is a chance to cast our burdens and cares at his feet.

We pray to seek his wisdom so that we can learn to walk in the way he has for us to go.

We pray to find comfort and peace so that we can have a sound mind.

We pray to obtain healing, whether it is for our heart or for our physical body.

We pray for help! For we know not what to do, but we go to him in confidence because he knows all: the situation, the people or things involved, and all the details. And he knows what is best and what is needed.

We need to know that God answers our prayers and trust his timing. He may answer with a yes, no, or not now. And because our prayers usually involve more than just us, we need to trust he is working out all things for our good in his time.

We also need to remember God is not Santa Claus. He is not here to just give us great gifts, not that he doesn't give great gifts because he does. As a matter of fact, he gave us the greatest gift of all, his Son, who died on the cross so that we would have eternal life.

> For God so loved the world that he gave his
> one and only Son, that whoever believes in him
> shall not perish but have eternal life. (John 3:16
> NIV)

Perhaps the second greatest gift was when the curtain tore in two in the temple as Jesus gave his life on the cross. As a result, we know we now have direct access to God. No longer are we separated from him.

> And when Jesus had cried out again in a
> loud voice, he gave up his spirit. At that moment
> the curtain of the temple was torn in two from
> top to bottom. The earth shook, the rocks split.
> (Matthew 27:50–51 NIV)

We need to realize that God is not a genie. He does not grant our every wish, such as a big house or a winning lottery ticket. Nor does he override another person's will to make us happy. No, God knows what we need. He knows what we can handle. And he knows what is best for us. If he gave us everything we asked for, we would probably not learn good work ethics or be able to appreciate the things we have in life or learn how to deal with or solve problems. God is not about making sure we are happy all the time. He is about making us the best version of ourselves as he transforms us into his likeness.

The most important thing we can do is go to his throne room. When we enter, we need to believe we are coming before God himself. We begin by imagining ourselves approaching God's throne room. As we come before him, we come with a humble heart, ready to say, "Here I am, Lord, speak to me," or, "Lord, I have so much to say to you, please listen to me as my heart is heavy, and I need your peace and direction." Invite God into the room and into your heart. Ask God to fill you with his Holy Spirit. Be authentic, be truthful, and tell him how you are feeling.

The more you believe you are before God, the more you start to know you are before him. The more you know you are before him, the more you will feel his presence and hear his voice.

Questions

1) Reread Psalm 25:9. Who does God guide? What does God guide them in?

____

____

2) What are some things you can do to have the right mind-set when you are meeting with God?

____

____

3) What does a humble and right heart look like?

____

____

4) Why is it important to go to God with the right intentions?

____

____

5)   How do you see God as you enter the throne room?

____

____

6)   What are you seeking from your prayer time with God?

____

____

For Reflection

- We go to God expecting to meet with him.
- We enter the throne room with a humble heart.
- We enter the throne room for the right reason.
- God teaches the humble his ways.
- God answers our prayers with yes, no, or not now.
- We need to trust God is working out all things for our good in his time.

Prayer to Approach God's Throne Room

Heavenly Father,

Here I am, Lord Jesus, be near. I come to your throne room seeking you and wanting to draw close to you. Lord, I invite you into this place and ask you to fill it with your presence. Fill me, Lord, with your Holy Spirit. For I want to know you and learn to walk in your ways. Give me a heart like yours, Lord, one that loves others and has patience, compassion, and understanding. Give me eyes to see you, Lord, and eyes to see what you see in others. Lord, give me ears to hear you as you speak to me and direct my steps. Help me to walk in obedience to your Word. Lord, help me to be more like you with each passing day so that you can be glorified by my behavior.

In Jesus's name I pray.

Amen.

CHAPTER 4

Moved to My Knees

It is written, "As surely as I live," says the Lord, "every knee
will bow before me; every tongue will confess to God."

—Romans 14:11 (BSB)

One morning I was sitting on the porch at our cottage on the Chesapeake Bay and I was doing my daily reading of the Bible. I was in the Old Testament reading about King Solomon. He had just finished building the temple to the Lord, and he was getting ready to pray for the dedication of it.

> Then Solomon stood before the altar of the Lord in front of the whole assembly of Israel and spread out his hands. Now he had made a bronze platform, five cubits long, five cubits wide, and three cubits high and placed it in the center of the outer court. He stood on the platform and then knelt down before the whole assembly of Israel and spread out his hands toward heaven. (2 Chronicles 6:12–13 NIV)

Then I heard a voice say, "Did you see that?"

I said, "What?" I read the passage again, and again the voice said,

"Did you see that?" right after I read, "He stood on the platform and then knelt down."

I said, "That he knelt down?"

"Yes," the voice said. Then the voice said, "How many times have you prayed on your knees?" I began to recall each time on my fingers. Then the voice said, "And what happened each time you prayed on your knees?"

As I began to recall the times I had prayed on my knees, I replied, "Oh, wow." I remember that each time, as they were few, they were powerful times.

The voice said, "If there were a king or queen here, would you not show respect and bow before them?"

"Yes," I said.

He quickly brought to mind an image of a prisoner on his knees surrendering. I felt the Lord was telling me I needed to go to him with a surrendered heart. Then another image came to my mind. It was of a man on one knee asking a woman to marry him. Just as that man out of his love for her submitted to the woman, I felt God was showing me that out of my love for him, I too should submit to God's will for my life.

I immediately put my Bible down and went in our bedroom. As I began to go on my knees I was reminded of when Moses came to the burning bush in Exodus 3:5 and God called out to him and said, "Do not come any closer. Take off your sandals, for the place where you are standing is holy ground." I quickly took my sandals off and knelt down on my knees and began to weep and pray. I began by confessing that I had gotten complacent with my prayer life. I was getting way too comfortable praying in my favorite chair or my car, anywhere and everywhere, but on my knees.

That was the day my prayer life changed forever. God graciously and gently reminded me that it is a privilege and honor to come before him. I began incorporating kneeling for my morning prayer time out of reverence for God. More importantly, I took on a new posture of my heart. I started to surrender my plans to God instead of holding on to what I thought should happen and submitted to his will for my life, trusting his plan is for my good.

> Moses and Aaron went from the assembly to the entrance of the tent of meeting and fell facedown, and the glory of the Lord appeared to them. (Numbers 20:6 NIV)

> Three times a day he [Daniel] got down on his knees and prayed, giving thanks to his God, just as he had done before. (Daniel 6:10 NIV)

> Come let us bow down in worship, let us kneel before the Lord our Maker. (Psalm 95:6 NIV)

> Surrender your heart to God, turn to him in prayer. (Job 11:13 NIV)

> Submit yourselves, then, to God. (James 4:7 NIV)

> Do not merely listen to the word, and so deceive yourselves. Do what it says. (James 1:22 NIV)

Questions

1) Reread Numbers 20:6. How did Moses and Aaron respond when the Lord appeared to them?

____

____

2) What was it that the psalmist encouraged those that worshiped God to do in Psalm 95:6?

____

____

3) Reread 2 Chronicles 6:13. How did King Solomon show reverence as he dedicated the temple to God?

____

____

4) What does Job 11:13 tell us to do?

____

____

5) What does James tell us to do in James 4:7?

____

____

6) What other advice does James give us in James 1:22?

____

____

7) Are you willing to submit and surrender to God's will for your life?

____

____

8) What areas in your life are hard for you to surrender and submit to God? Why?

____

____

For Reflection

- Come to God in whatever position expresses your humble heart in reverence to him.
- We need to surrender to God and let go of control.
- We need to submit to God's will and trust his plans for our lives.
- We need to not just read and listen to God's Word but do as it says.

Prayer

Heavenly Father,

Who am I to be able to come before your holy throne?

Lord, I ask your forgiveness for those times when I have been complacent in my prayer time with you. For you, Lord, are worthy of my respect and honor.

Help me, Lord, to approach your throne in a way that best positions me to come with a humble heart and a heart that submits to your will. Help me, Lord, to surrender all my plans, trusting that your plans are the best for me. Give me a heart that is also willing not to just hear, but give me a heart to do what you say so I may live a life in obedience to your Word.

In Jesus's name I pray.

Amen.

PART 2

Praying With Purpose

CHAPTER 5

How We Are to Pray

But when you pray, go into your room, close the
door and pray to your Father, who is unseen.

—Matthew 6:6 (NIV)

There is no one right way to pray. In fact, there are several ways to approach God. The important thing is to pray.

One way is to pray short little prayers throughout your day, such as "Help me, Lord," "Give me strength," "Give me wisdom, Lord," "Give me direction, Lord," "Take away this fear, Lord," "Renew my mind, Lord," "Help me to feel better, Lord," "Give me words to speak, Lord," or "Give me patience, Lord." I'm sure these sound pretty familiar, and they are appropriate during the busyness of our days. But we also need to set aside quality time in prayer where we pour out our hearts to the Lord.

Another way to pray, which I particularly like, is to read a scripture verse and then turn that verse into a prayer.

For example:

Whether you turn to the right or to the left,
your ears will hear a voice behind you, saying,
"This is the way; walk in it." (Isaiah 30:21 NIV)

Heavenly Father,

You are my strength when I'm weak, and you are the one that gives me courage when I am fearful. You are the one I look to for guidance, so help me, Lord, to hear your voice as you tell me, "This is the way, walk in it."

Help me not to be so set on where I think I should go that I miss hearing you. Help me, Lord, to be obedient to the way you would have me go, having faith, courage, and trust that this is what is good for me. Help me, as I surrender all to you, Lord!

In Jesus's name I pray.
Amen.

Yet another way to pray is to follow the example Jesus gave to his disciples when they asked him how they should pray. We all know his response as the Lord's Prayer.

I always start my morning reading God's Word, and then I spend time on my knees in prayer. This is when I have my quality prayer time. The format I use is similar to that used by many small groups. It incorporates all the parts of the Lord's Prayer, and it's easy to remember: PARTS (praise, adoration, repentance, thanksgiving, supplication). Some people use ACTS (adoration, confession, thanksgiving, supplication) as their guide. Both accomplish the same goal.

Questions

1) Reread Matthew 6:6. What does Jesus say we should do when we pray?

____

____

2)   Who does Jesus say we are to pray to?

____

____

3)   What is the example Jesus gave to his disciples?

____

____

4)   In what ways do you pray?

____

____

For Reflection

- Pray.
- Pray to an unseen Father.
- Pray short prayers.
- Pray using scripture.
- Pray using PARTS.

Prayer on How We Are to Pray

Heavenly Father,

As I look outside today, I am struck by all the beauty in your creation. Lord, how I *praise* your mighty work.

Lord, empty me of all my *sins* and create in me a clean heart. Give me a willing spirit, Lord, to walk in all your ways.

Thank you, Lord, for the new beginnings today brings. Thank you for your amazing love and blessings in my life. Thank you that when I seek you and call upon your name, you hear me. Thank you for your word and truth.

Lord, I *ask* that you would lead me this day in your will for me. Help me to have clarity in all the decisions that need to be made. Help me to walk in the path you have for me with confidence, faith, trust, and courage, knowing that your plan is for my good. May my life reflect you and bring glory to your name.

In Jesus's name I pray.

Amen.

CHAPTER 6

Adoration and Praise to Our God

> Through Jesus, therefore, let us continually
> offer to God a sacrifice of praise—the fruit
> of lips that openly profess his name.
>
> —Hebrews 13:15 (NIV)

Why do we need to praise God? He certainly doesn't need us to praise or adore him even though his Word tells us to do so. No, adoration helps us to remember who he is. It is a time of worship. Praise helps us remember what he has done.

Another reason to begin prayer by praising God is that Jesus taught his disciples to begin that way in the Lord's Prayer: "Our Father who art in heaven, hallowed be thy name" (Matthew 6: 9 NIV).

In the book of Psalm, you see many verses of praise written by King David, Solomon, Moses, Asaph (one of the three temple singers assigned by David), and others.

Verses of Praise and Adoration from the Book of Psalm

> I will praise you, O LORD, with all my
> heart; I will tell of all your wonders. I will be glad

and rejoice in you; I will sing praise to your name
O Most High. (Psalm 9:1–2 NIV)

> Your love, Lord, reaches to the heavens, your faithfulness to the skies. Your righteousness is like the highest mountains, your justice like the great deep. (Psalm 36:5–6 NIV)

> LORD, you have been our dwelling place throughout all generations. Before the mountains were born or you brought forth the earth and the world, from everlasting to everlasting you are God. (Psalm 90:1–2 NIV)

Let your quality prayer time begin with one of the praise and adoration verses from the psalmists who eloquently worshipped God or choose to praise him for what he is doing or has done in your own life.

Another way to begin prayer is to start with worship music. Let those words be your praise to God.

Questions

1) Reread Hebrews 13:15. What does the scripture say we should continually offer?

____

____

2) For what reasons do you think we should praise God?

____

____

3) What words would you use to describe who God is?

____

____

4) What things in your own life has God done for you that you want to praise him for?

____

____

5) Take time now to praise God for what he is doing or has done in your life.

____

____

For Reflection

- Adoration and praise are a time of worship.
- Adoration helps us remember who God is.
- Praise helps us remember what God has done.

Prayers of Praise from Scripture

Heavenly Father,

"Great is the LORD and most worthy of praise; his greatness no one can fathom. One generation commends your works to another; they tell of your mighty acts. They speak of the glorious splendor of your majesty, and I will meditate on your wonderful works" (Psalm 145:3–5 NIV).

Yes, Lord, I will speak of your glorious splendor and will tell my children and their children of your mighty work in my life. For I want them to know the God that I serve and praise. For you are a God filled with love and compassion. You are a Father that provides for your children, and you are a God that I want them to know and walk with. How great is our God! You, Lord, are worthy to be praised.

In Jesus's name I pray.

Amen.

*****

Heavenly Father,

"Worship the LORD with gladness; come before him with joyful songs. Know that the LORD is God. It is he who made us, and we are his; we are his people, the sheep of his pasture. Enter his gates with thanksgiving and his courts with praise; give thanks to him and praise his name" (Psalm 100:2–4 NIV).

Father God, I do praise your holy name, and as I enter your courts this morning to seek you and spend time with you, I say thank you and praise you.

Thank you for being my Creator. Thank you that I am a child of God. Thank you that I can come to you and you hear my prayers. Thank you that you are never too busy for me, and thank you that I can trust you. For you are faithful always and your plans for me are for my good. So I will worship you with gladness!

In Jesus's name I pray.

Amen.

CHAPTER 7

Confessing and Turning from Our Sins

If we confess our sins, he is faithful and just and will forgive
us our sins, and purify us from all unrighteousness.

—1 John 1:9 (NIV)

Unconfessed sin separates us from God. So it is important that
we confess our sins daily in order for our prayers to be effective.
We see this confession demonstrated in the Lord's Prayer:

And forgive us our trespasses as we forgive
them that trespass against us. (Matthew 6: 12
NMB)

King David wrote Psalm 51 after Nathan the prophet exposed
David's sin of adultery against Bathsheba and murder against her
husband, Uriah. Note how David asks God to cleanse him from his
sin in the following passages.

Have mercy on me, O God, according to
your unfailing love; according to your great compassion blot out my transgressions. Wash away all
my iniquity and cleanse me from my sin. (Psalm
51:1–2 NIV)

> Hide your face from my sins and blot out all
> my iniquity. Create in me a pure heart, O God,
> and renew a steadfast spirit within me. Do not
> cast me from your presence or take your Holy
> Spirit from me. Restore to me the joy of your
> salvation and grant me a willing spirit, to sustain
> me. (Psalm 51:9–12 NIV)

Above all we need to guard our hearts. By that I mean make sure you are careful to live according to God's Word. And when we do sin, we need to confess it immediately. Keeping short accounts with God prevents Satan from gaining a foothold in our lives, separating us from God.

As we confess our sins we also need to repent and turn away from those sins so that we are set free from the weight of our sin and can have a healthy soul.

I love how my pastor one day described sin.

Sin simply means missing the mark. I like the sound of that better than the word *sin*. I, for one, miss the mark constantly. We all do. None are perfect. That's why God sent his Son to die on the cross for us.

Having not grown up in the church and coming to the Lord as an adult, I had sinned much over the years. So Luke 7:47 aptly describes why I love our Lord so much: He forgave me much!

> Therefore I say to you, her sins, which are
> many, are forgiven, for she loved much; but he
> who is forgiven little, loves little. (Luke 7:47
> Amplified Bible)

Questions

1) Reread 1 John 1:9. What happens if we confess our sins?

____

____

2) Reread Mathew 6:12. What does Jesus say we should do when we ask for his forgiveness?

____

____

3) Reread Psalm 51:1–2. What does David ask God to do?

____

____

4) Reread Psalm 51:9–12. What does David ask God to do in this passage?

____

____

5) Do you have any sins to confess to God? Take a couple of minutes to ask the Lord to forgive you.

____

____

For Reflection

- Sin is simply missing the mark.
- Confess your sin. Keep short accounts with God. Harboring sin and wrong attitudes in our heart hinders our prayers.
- We confess our sins so that God can purify us and renew us with a steadfast spirit.
- We confess our sins to prevent the enemy from gaining a foothold into our heart and separating us from God.
- We need to not only confess our sins; we need to repent and turn away from those sins.
- Confession and repentance allow us to be free from the weight of sin and help us maintain a healthy soul.

Prayers for Confessing and Turning from Our Sins

Heavenly Father,

I come before you and ask that you cleanse me, Lord, of all that is unclean. Wash away all my sins. Lord, help me not to repeat my sin but repent and do what is right before you. Lord, restore to me the joy of your salvation and grant me a willing spirit to sustain me.

In Jesus's name I pray.

Amen.

*****

Heavenly Father,

I ask for your forgiveness for the times I misspoke by gossip or slander, instead of edifying and encouraging others. I also ask forgiveness for the times I was silent and did not speak about your great love or share the gospel.

Lord, forgive me for misrepresenting you by my actions or speech.

Lord, I ask that you use me to spread your Word and your truth. Help me to leave a legacy that will encourage future generations to draw closer to your throne room.

Help me, Lord, to finish what you have started in me.

In Jesus's name I pray.

Amen.

CHAPTER 8

A Heart of Thanksgiving

Thanks be to God for his indescribable gift.

—2 Corinthians 9:15 (NIV)

Growing up we were taught to say thank you when someone gave us something, whether it was a drink, a gift, or a compliment. We were told that it is the polite thing to do and it shows gratitude for their kindness.

How much more should we say thank you to our God? For each day is a gift filled with blessings. We just need to open our eyes to see them. Giving thanks helps us to focus on the good things in our lives and to remind us who gave us these blessings, which James does in the following scripture:

> Every good and perfect gift is from above, coming down from the Father of the heavenly lights, who does not change like shifting shadows. (James 1:17 NIV)

Isaiah also tells us to give thanks.

> And on that day you will say, 'Give thanks to the LORD, call on His name. Make known His

deeds among the peoples; Make them remember that His name is exalted.' Praise the LORD in song, for He has done glorious things; Let this be known throughout the earth. (Isaiah 12:4–5 NASB)

God also goes one step further and asks us to give thanks in all circumstances, not just for the good gifts we receive but through the rough times as well. Rejoice always, pray continually, give thanks in all circumstance; for this is God's will for you in Christ Jesus. (1 Thessalonians 5:16–18 NIV)

This one was hard for me. I remember God showing me scriptures about giving thanks in all circumstances and saying in another to consider it all joy. I felt he was telling me to start saying thank you. I remember telling God that I didn't want to, that everything that was going on in my life was difficult; it was too hard, and it hurt too much to say thank you. But I decided to do it out of obedience to him. I began with the basics. "Thank you, Lord, for loving me, and thank you for this day." As I began the practice of giving thanks, it became easier. "Thank you that I'm not alone; thank you that you are with me, Lord. Thank you that you are working in this situation, and thank you, Lord, for helping me to start seeing you in the midst of this storm."

I just want to stop right now and say, "Thank you, Lord, for helping me understand how important it is to practice giving thanks in all circumstances."

Giving thanks to God through the hard times allowed me to focus on what he was doing in the situation and who he is, instead of focusing on the hurt and pain I was feeling. This opened my eyes to seeing how God was working through the storm in my life.

Consider it all joy, my brethren, when you encounter various trials, knowing that the testing of your faith produces endurance. (James 1:2–3 NASB 1995)

Questions

1) Why do you think we need to thank God?

____

____

2) Reread Isaiah 12:4–5. What does Isaiah tell us to do? What are we supposed to make known?

____

____

3) Reread 1 Thessalonians 5:16–18. What three things are we told to do?

____

____

4) Why do you think God asks us to say thank you in the difficult times?

____

____

5) What do you think God means when he says in James 1:3, "The testing of your faith produces endurance?"

____

____

6) Why is it so hard to say thank you in the difficult times of our lives?

____

____

7) Looking back to difficult times in your life, what are some things that you can now say thank you for?

____

____

For Reflection

- Give thanks to God for our blessings.
- Give thanks to God in all circumstances, even the difficult times.
- Remember the testing of your faith produces endurance.

Prayer for Thanksgiving

Heavenly Father,

You tell us in Colossians 4:2, "Devote yourselves to prayer, being watchful and thankful."

So I come before you in prayer today to say thank you!

Thank you, Lord, for all that you have done in my life, the roof over my head, the shoes on my feet, the clothes on my back, and the food on my table.

Thank you for loving me despite all my flaws and lack of faith.

Thank you, Lord, for never giving up on me, even when I have felt like giving up.

Thank you for hearing my prayers and for answering them in your perfect way.

Thank you for your Word that ministers to my heart.

Thank you for your Son who died on the cross so that my debt is paid for and my sins are forgiven.

Thank you that I am no longer separated from you but made clean and right. Thank you for my salvation.

Thank you that I am a child of God!

In Jesus's name I pray.

Amen.

CHAPTER 9

Coming Before the Lord in Supplication

The prayer of a righteous man is powerful and effective.

—James 5:16b (NIV)

Supplication is when we come before the Lord with our prayer requests. We see this modeled in the Lord's Prayer: "Give us this day our daily bread" (Matthew 6:11 NMB).

This is our time to cast our burdens on the Lord as we go to the throne room. It's a time to be honest with God—even about how we feel. It's okay to admit that you're mad, you're hurt, or you're scared. God already knows how we feel, but telling him allows him to help us with those feelings.

Know that this time with him is precious and holy. We are talking to the Great I Am. Not only are we talking to him, but he is listening to us!

> Then you will call on me and come and pray to me, and I will listen to you. (Jeremiah 29:12 NIV)

When we think of prayer, we need to look at Jesus and the great example he showed us in the garden of Gethsemane.

> Then Jesus went with his disciples to a place called Gethsemane, and he said to them, "Sit here while I go over there and pray." (Matthew 26:36 NIV)

> Going a little farther, he fell with his face to the ground and prayed, "My Father, if it is possible, may this cup be taken from me. Yet not as I will, but as you will." (Matthew 26:39 NIV)

There have been many times in my life that I have found myself in pain and agony over what was going on in my life or others' lives. I know that those times cannot even begin to compare to what Jesus was feeling and going through that night, but I do know how helpless I felt and the excruciating pain I was feeling. Just as Jesus said, "May this cup be taken from me," I too have cried out that same plea for myself or others.

But as I cried out, I know the only thing I could do was surrender like Jesus, "Yet not as I will, but as You will." I needed to trust God's plan and his timing. I needed to be aligned with God's will; that was the only way to get through it.

> This is the confidence we have in approaching God: that if we ask anything according to his will, he hears us. (1 John 5:14 NIV)

Questions

1) Reread James 5:16. What does it say about the prayer of a righteous man?

____

____

2) Reread Jeremiah 29:12. What happens when we call on God and come and pray?

____

____

3) Reread Matthew 26:39. What did Jesus ask the Father to do? What did Jesus say after that?

____

____

4) What are some things that you need to take to the throne room?

____

____

For Reflection

- Supplication is when we go to God to cast our cares and burdens at his throne.
- Be honest with God on how you feel and ask him to help you with those feelings.
- Surrender all to God.
- Ask God to align your thoughts with his will.

Prayers Incorporating Praise, Adoration, Repentance, Thanksgiving, and Supplication (PARTS)

Heavenly Father,

Oh, how I *praise* your holy name! For you, Lord, are my rock and my strength.

Father God, I come before you to *confess* my sins. Empty me, Lord, of my judgmental ways and my thoughts that are not right before you. Cover my iniquities and create in me a clean heart and renew a right spirit in me.

Thank you, Lord, for your grace! Thank you, Lord, for your amazing love. Thank you, Lord Jesus, for what you did on the cross, for by your wounds and your shed blood I am healed and made right before the Father. Thank you, Lord, for eternal life, and thank you for your Word, your truth.

Lord, *guide me* this day in all that I do! Help me to feel your presence; I know you are with me. Lord, help me to walk in your ways so that others would see you in me and glorify your name.

In Jesus's name I pray.

Amen.

*****

Heavenly Father,

How awesome are you, Lord! How I *praise* your name! Lord, I come before you to seek your face, to draw near to you, Lord, so that I may feel your holy presence.

Father God, empty me of all that is ugly before you. Help me, Lord, to *repent* and turn from those ways so that I may be made clean and no longer carry the weight of my sins.

Thank you, Lord, for loving me despite all my flaws. Thank you that you will never leave me nor forsake me. Thank you, Lord, that your arms are always open wide ready to receive me and your ears are attentive to my voice.

Lord, you said in Isaiah 58:11, "The LORD will guide you always; he will satisfy your needs in a sun-scorched land and will strengthen your frame. You will be like a well-watered garden, like a spring whose waters never fail."

Lord, *guide me* this day in all that I do. Satisfy my needs, Lord, for you know what I need. Strengthen my frame, Lord—my mind, heart, soul, and body—so that I will be strong in you. Help me to be like a well-watered garden, a spring whose waters never fail.

In Jesus's name I pray.

Amen.

CHAPTER 10

The Righteous Cry Out

The righteous cry out, and the LORD hears them;
he delivers them from all their troubles.

—Psalm 34:17 (NIV)

There are times when our hearts are full of hurt and pain and our minds are overwhelmed and unable to process what is going on. We just can't believe the news we just heard. It can happen in an instant: one phone call, one accident, or one storm, and our lives can be turned upside down. It could be the loss of a job, a loved one in an accident, a marriage or relationship ending, a miscarriage, or the words you or a loved one has cancer. Our physical body just collapse, and our hearts begin to pound out of our chests as our minds cry out, "Why? What happened? How?"

Unfortunately, there will be a time in each one of our lives that we will have trouble. Jesus warns us of this, but he also tells us to remain in him and we will have peace no matter what our trouble is.

"I [Jesus] have told you these things, so that
in me you may have peace. In this world you will
have trouble. But take heart! I have overcome the
world." (John 16:33 NIV)

In December 2020, I remember getting the call from my youngest son, Christopher, with the news that his doctor just told him he had stage 4 cancer. I remember keeping it together saying to my son, "We can beat this. You got this. God is a God of miracles."

As I hung up the phone and muttered the unbelievable news to my husband, I felt like all the air was taken out of me. I remember we had a maintenance person at our house fixing something, and I said to my husband, "I just need to go in the other room and pray to God." He nodded and I went.

I fell to the ground on my knees and began crying out to the Lord. I think I prayed and cited every verse I could think of starting with Psalm 34:17, "The righteous cry out," to somewhere in the middle praying Mark 11:24, "Therefore I tell you, whatever you ask for in prayer, believe that you have received it, and it will be yours," to ending with Matthew 19:26, "With God all things are possible," and Matthew 26:39, "May this cup be taken from Christopher, yet not as I will, but as you will."

God's Word just kept flooding my mind as I prayed, and tears rolled down my face. At this point, I'm so glad I worked on memorizing scripture. For it is times like this we cling to God's Word.

I got up off the floor and knew I needed more than just me and my husband praying, so I sent an e-mail to my prayer-warrior friends telling them the news and enlisting their help with prayer.

Throughout this journey there were some difficult times in which I knew I needed more help than my friends could provide. I reached out to a dedicated prayer group that I belonged to, and within the first hour of sending the request out, there were over a thousand people praying for Christopher. I remember tears of thankfulness and gratitude coming down my face as I thanked and praised God for all these people that didn't know me or Christopher but took the time to stop and pray and petition God for healing. Oh, how that filled my heart with hope and encouragement.

I remained faithful to pray daily, and God showered me with his love through visions, songs, signs, and scripture along the journey. I eagerly shared it all with Christopher. I wanted him to see what God was showing me so he could be encouraged as well. I held on to a vision I had. It was about Mother's Day, and I opened the door, and it was Christopher, and he was all healthy and healed and we hugged. Short and sweet. This vision happened within the first few days of Christopher's diagnosis. I held on tight and never lost sight of that vision and even used it to remind God of what he showed me.

Each time I drove Christopher to chemo, there were certain songs that kept coming on the radio that let us know everything was going to be okay. I would sing some of the lyrics at the top of my voice and remind Christopher that it was going to be okay.

I say all this so that you too will look for the signs. I don't want you to miss any signs God has for you along the way of your journey. These are the things that continue to give us hope and encouragement and let us know God is hearing us and working things out.

My boldness in prayer was based on the fact that Jesus's blood made me righteous and thereby eligible to cry out and know that he heard me.

> God made him who had no sin to be sin for us, so that in him we might become the righteousness of God. (2 Corinthians 5:21 NIV)

> So, now that we have been made righteous by his [Jesus] blood, we can be even more certain that we will be saved from God's wrath through him. (Romans 5:9 CEB)

Questions

1) Reread 2 Corinthians 5:21. Who are the righteous ones?

____

____

2) Reread Romans 5:9. Why are we made righteous in Christ?

____

____

3) Now that you know you are made righteous, does that make you feel different going to God's throne room? If so, how?

____

____

4) Reread John 16:33. Why do you think Jesus told you that you will have trouble in this world?

____

____

5) Think of a time when you were the righteous one crying out. Were there signs to help you along the way?

____

____

6) What became of your prayer life as you were going through this difficult time?

____

____

7) Who are the people you know and can enlist for prayer?

____

____

For Reflection

- You will have troubles in this world.
- You are made righteous by Christ's blood shed on the cross.
- The righteous cry out, so remain faithful in *prayer* and reading God's Word.
- Enlist people to pray; join prayer groups.
- Memorize and personalize scripture to make it yours.
- Look for encouraging signs from God after you have prayed.

Prayer of the Righteous Crying Out

Heavenly Father,

My heart is overwhelmed, filled with hurt and pain. My mind is still processing why, what, and how this is happening. Lord, your Word says the righteous cry out and the Lord hears us and delivers us from all our troubles. Lord, I cry out and ask for you to hear me and to deliver us from this trouble.

Your Word, Lord, also says, "In this world you will have troubles." You say that you tell us these things so that in you, Jesus, we will have peace. Lord, I ask for that peace.

Lord, may wisdom enter my heart and knowledge be pleasant to my soul as I try to understand your ways, which are higher than mine. I look for your wisdom, which is a treasure, so that it can guide me.

Lord, hear the cry of my heart and deliver us.
In Jesus's name I pray.
Amen.

PART 3

Moving Forward in Prayer

CHAPTER 11

Put on the Armor of God

Finally, be strong in the Lord and in his mighty
power. Put on the full armor of God, so that you can
take your stand against the devil's schemes.

—Ephesians 6:10–11 (NIV)

We need to realize that there is an enemy out there who wants to separate us from God, and he does not play fair. He lies. He wants to rob us of our joy in the Lord, and he also wants to destroy our relationship with him.

The enemy usually comes when we least expect it. He can work through strangers, family members, work associates, and friends. Nothing and no one are off-limits to Satan. A great example of this is when Judas, one of Jesus own disciples, betrayed him.

Then Satan entered Judas, called Iscariot,
one of the Twelve. And Judas went to the chief
priest and the officers of the temple guard and
discussed with them how he might betray Jesus.
(Luke 22:3–4 NIV)

He knows our weaknesses and where we are most vulnerable. He will attack our relationships, our jobs, our health, and our finances. He will sneak his way into our lives, trying to wreak havoc in our minds and hearts until he gets you where he wants you: not trusting God, isolated, and fearful. He will keep trying until he succeeds unless you put on the armor of God and stand strong in his mighty power.

So put on the full armor of God as described in the following scriptures so that you can be protected from the enemy and his schemes.

> For our struggle is not against flesh and blood but against the rulers, against the authorities, against the powers of this dark world and spiritual forces of evil in the heavenly realms. Therefore put on the full armor of God, so that when the day of evil comes, you may be able to stand your ground, and after you have done everything, to stand. Stand firm then, with the belt of truth buckled around your waist, with the breastplate of righteousness in place, and with your feet fitted with the readiness that comes from the gospel of peace. In addition to all this, take up the shield of faith, with which you can extinguish all the flaming arrows of the evil one. Take the helmet of salvation and the sword of the Spirit, which is the word of God. And pray in the Spirit on all occasions with all kinds of prayers and requests. With this in mind, be alert and always keep on praying for all the saints. (Ephesians 6:12–18 NIV)

> The thief comes only to steal and kill and destroy; I came that they may have life, and have it abundantly. (John 10:10 ESV)

> Again, the devil took him [Jesus] to a very high mountain and showed him all the

Kingdoms of the world and their splendor. "All this I will give you," he said, "if you will bow down and worship me." Jesus said to him, "Away from me, Satan! For it is written: Worship the Lord your God, and serve him only." Then the devil left him, and angels came and attended him. (Matthew 4:8–11 NIV)

Questions

1) Reread Ephesians 6:10–11. Why do we put on the armor of God?

\
\

2) Reread Ephesians 6:12–18. Who is our struggle with?

\
\

3) What are the parts of the armor described in Ephesians 6:12–18? What is the purpose of each one?

\
\

4) What is our only offensive weapon in the armor of God? How are we to use it?

\
\

5) Reread John 10:10. Why does the thief come? Why did Jesus come?

\
\

6) Reread Matthew 4:8–11. What was the devil trying to accomplish? How did Jesus respond?

____

____

7) When have you felt the enemy attacking? What did you do?

____

____

For Reflection

- Be aware of the enemy.
- Put on the armor of God.
- Remember Jesus came so we can have life and have it abundantly.
- Pray and use your sword, God's Word, to battle the enemy.
- Rebuke the enemy!
- When tempted Jesus quoted scripture and said, "Away from me, Satan! It is written," and the devil left him.
- Memorize scripture.
- The enemy knows our weakness and where we are vulnerable, so be prepared.

Prayer for Putting on the Armor of God

Heavenly Father,

I come in prayer because it feels like the enemy is all around me, ready to pounce on me. Lord, help me to be strong in you and in your mighty power.

Help me, Lord, to put on your full armor so that I can be protected from the enemy's schemes. Help me to stand firm in your truth as I put the belt around my waist. Make sure I put on my breastplate of righteousness and help fit me with the feet of peace, your gospel.

Lord, help me to take up the shield of faith and not waiver in it so that I can extinguish the arrows of the devil. Lord, help me remember my helmet of salvation and lift up high my sword of the spirit and speak your Word as Jesus himself did.

Lord, may all the plans of the enemy boomerang on him as I rebuke the enemy and say, "Flee in the name of Jesus!"

In Jesus's name I pray.

Amen.

CHAPTER 12

Standing Firm in Your Faith

If you do not stand firm in your faith,
you will not stand at all.

—Isaiah 7:9 (NIV)

The very core and foundation of Christianity is based on faith—believing that Jesus is God's Son, believing that Jesus died for our sins, believing Jesus rose from the grave and conquered death, believing we are forgiven for our sins, believing we have eternal life, believing in God's love, believing in what we do not see!

Now faith is being sure of what we hope for
and certain of what we do not see. (Hebrews 11:1
NIV)

We see so many examples of people in the Bible that are commended for their faith. By faith Noah built the ark. Abraham, when called by God, moved to the Promised Land and believed he would have a child with Sarah, even though Sarah was barren and past the age of having a child. By faith Moses went to Egypt to get Pharaoh to let the Israelites leave Egypt. By faith the Israelites passed through the Red Sea. By faith Shadrach, Meshach, and Abednego did not bow down to worship the image of gold that Nebuchadnezzar had built. But instead, they had faith that God could rescue them from the burning furnace. Daniel, by faith, continued to pray to God even though it meant he would be thrown into the den of lions. The list goes on and on.

"And without faith it is impossible to please God, because anyone who comes to him must believe that he exists and that he rewards those who earnestly seek him" (Hebrews 11:6 NIV).

We are told by Jesus that all we need is faith as small as a mustard seed, nothing grand but something as small as a mustard seed. I don't know about you, but I find that reassuring as there are times in my life that I feel that is all I have.

> He [Jesus] replied, "If you have faith as small as a mustard seed, you can say to this mulberry tree, 'Be uprooted and planted in the sea' and it will obey you." (Luke 17:6 NIV)

In the Gospel of Mark, Jesus expanded on the importance of faith in prayer.

> "Have faith in God," Jesus answered. "Truly I tell you, if anyone says to this mountain, 'Go throw yourself into the sea,' and does not doubt in their heart but believes that what they say will happen, it will be done for them. Therefore I tell you, whatever you ask for in prayer, believe that you have received it, and it will be yours." (Mark 11:22–24 NIV)

Questions

1) Reread Hebrews 11:1. What does it say faith is?

____

____

2) Reread Mark 11:22–24. What size of faith does Jesus say we need to have? What does Jesus say we need to do as we come in prayer?

____

____

3) Reread Hebrews 11:6. What do we need to have to please God? What two things must we come to God with?

____

____

4) Reread Isaiah 7:9. What does the verse mean and how would you apply it?

____

____

For Reflection

- Stand firm in your faith.
- We only need faith as small as a mustard seed.
- Do not let your heart doubt.
- It is impossible to please God without faith.

Prayer for Faith

Heavenly Father,

I'm so thankful that all I need is faith as small as a mustard seed. Lord, I cling to that and ask that you continue to help my faith grow. For I know without faith, it is impossible to please you. Help my heart not to doubt what I do not see, but instead help me to stand even firmer in my faith, trusting and believing you hear my prayers and that you will answer them in the way that is best for me.

In Jesus's name I pray.

Amen.

CHAPTER 13

Trusting in the Lord

Trust in the Lord with all your heart. And do not lean on
your own understanding. In all your ways acknowledge
Him, and He will make your paths straight.

—Proverbs 3:5–6 (NASB 1995)

We live in a world where trust is hard to come by. I have had many
times where people, friends, and even family members have broken
trust. Because of those past hurts and disappointments, I have tended
to not let people close to me. At those times the Lord reminded me of
the passage above, which was the very first passage I memorized. It is
filled with such sound advice and helped me to understand that I was
putting my trust in the wrong place, in others instead of the Lord.
There is no better place than to put our trust in the Lord, for he is
our refuge in times of trouble and he will make our paths straight.

> But I trust in your unfailing love. I will
> rejoice because you have rescued me. (Psalm 13:5
> NLT)

> Those who trust in the LORD are like
> Mount Zion, which cannot be shaken but
> endures forever. (Psalm 125:1 NIV)

Trust in the LORD forever, because GOD the LORD is the Rock eternal. (Isaiah 26:4 BSB)

The LORD is good, a refuge in times of trouble. He cares for those who trust in him. (Nahum 1:7 NIV)

Questions

1) Reread Proverbs 3:5–6. How should we trust the Lord? What two things are we supposed to do as we trust in the Lord?

____

____

2) Reread Psalm 125:1. What happens to those that trust in the Lord?

____

____

3) Reread Isaiah 26:4. What is the name used for God?

____

____

4) Reread Nahum 1:7. How is the Lord referred to?

____

____

For Reflection

- We need to trust in the Lord with all our heart.
- We need to not lean on our own understanding.
- We need to acknowledge him.
- He cares for those who trust in him.

Prayer for Trusting in the Lord

Heavenly Father,
Oh, how I praise you, Lord!
Continue, Lord, to make my paths straight as I trust in you.
Help me, Lord, not to put my trust in things or other people but to put my trust in you, Lord, as you are my refuge in times of trouble.
In Jesus's name I pray.
Amen.

CHAPTER 14

Finding Hope in the Lord

We put our hope in the LORD. He is our help and
our shield. In him our hearts rejoice, for we trust
in his holy name. Let your unfailing love surround
us, LORD, for our hope is in you alone.

—Psalm 33:20–22 (NLT)

One night I was in my car driving and praying. When I finished my prayer, something caught my attention. It was a house with gigantic letters all lit up spelling the word *hope*. As I continued to drive, within a minute, I saw a cross lit up. I just began to weep and say, "Yes, Lord, my hope is in you! I got your sign!"

I don't know what challenges you are facing in your life now, but I do know that we need to put our hope in the Lord and trust he will see us through. We need to surrender whatever it is, letting go of what we hope will happen, and let God in. Trust that what he is going to do is for our good and that God's timing is always perfect.

May those who fear you rejoice when they
see me, for I have put my hope in your word.
(Psalm 119:74 NIV)

I wait for the LORD, my soul waits, and in his word I put my hope. (Psalm 130:5 NIV)

The Lord delights in those who fear him, who put their hope in his unfailing love. (Psalm 147:11 NIV)

But those who hope in the LORD will renew their strength. They will soar on wings like eagles; They will run and not grow weary, they will walk and not be faint. (Isaiah 40:31 NIV)

"For I know the plans I have for you," declares the LORD, "plans to prosper you and not to harm you, plans to give you hope and a future." (Jeremiah 29:11 NIV)

Questions

1) Reread Psalm 33:20–22. How does the psalmist describe who the Lord is?

____

____

2) Reread Psalm 119:74 and Psalm 130:5. What do the psalmists put their hope in?

____

____

3) Reread Psalm 147:11. What does the Lord delight in?

____

____

4)   Reread Isaiah 40:31. What happens to those who have hope in the Lord?

____

____

5)   Reread Jeremiah 29:11. How does this verse make you feel? Why?

____

____

For Reflection

- Put your hope in the Lord.
- The Lord is our help and our shield.
- We put our hope in his Word.
- Those who hope in the Lord will renew their strength.
- God has plans to give you hope and a future.

Prayers for Finding Hope in the Lord

Heavenly Father,

Praise be to the name of God forever and ever.

Lord, I come to you today to ask that you help me to overcome this anxiety, fear, and worry that I have.

Lord, help me to focus on you, your truth, and your faithfulness. When my mind begins to wonder and have negative or dark thoughts, help me to remember who you are. You, Lord, are the great I Am. You are the God that created the heavens above, the earth beneath, and the waters below. You are the one who put the stars in their place. You are the God that parted the Red Sea. You are the God of hope.

Help me to trust you, Lord, and remember that with you all things are possible.

Fill me, Lord, with all your joy and peace so that I may overflow with hope by the power of the Holy Spirit.

In Jesus's name I pray.
Amen.

*****

Heavenly Father,

"Lord, you alone are my portion and my cup; you make my lot secure" (Psalm 16:5 NIV).

Father God, thank you that you alone are my portion. I thank you that you are enough! Help me to keep my eyes always on you. For with you at my right hand, I will not be shaken. For you will not abandon me.

My hope is in you, Lord! Make known to me the path of life and fill me with joy in your presence.

In Jesus's name I pray.
Amen.

CHAPTER 15

A Life Filled With God's Peace

Peace I leave with you, my peace I give you. I do
not give to you as the world gives. Do not let your
hearts be troubled and do not be afraid.

—John 14:27 (NIV)

Growing up not knowing God's love and peace made it hard when faced with difficult circumstances. I was filled with worry, fear, and anxiety. I desperately desired to have peace but was unsure how to achieve it.

Years later, now that I am a Christian, I understand God's truth about his love and peace. As I read John 14:27 my heart is encouraged that God wants to replace our troubles and fears with his peace.

For God is not a God of disorder but of
peace—as in all the congregations of the Lord's
people. (1 Corinthians 14:33 NIV)

We all have days we need to be reminded of God's truth, that our God is a God of order and a God of peace. We just need to call upon his name and have faith as we ask for his peace that we will receive it.

Psalm 46:10 says, "Be still and know that I am God." We need only be still and have faith and trust in God. Our problems or fears are not going to automatically disappear, but at least we can find peace for our mind and soul as we come before his holy throne.

> The Lord gives strength to his people; the Lord blesses his people with peace. (Psalm 29:11 NIV)

> The mind governed by the flesh is death, but the mind governed by the Spirit is life and peace. (Romans 8:6 NIV)

> And the peace of God, which transcends all understanding, will guard your hearts and your minds in Christ Jesus. (Philippians 4:7 NIV)

Questions

1) Reread Psalm 29:11. What does the Lord give his people? What docs hc bless his people with?

____

____

2) Reread Romans 8:6. What does the mind governed by the flesh result in? What is the result governed by the Holy Spirit?

____

____

3) Reread 1 Corinthians 14:33. How is our God described?

____

____

4)   Reread Philippians 4:7. What type of peace does God give us?

____

____

For Reflection

- Christ leaves us with his peace.
- The Lord blesses his people with peace.
- God's peace transcends all understanding and guards our hearts and our minds.
- A mind governed by the flesh is death.
- A mind governed by the Holy Spirit is life and peace.

Prayer for Peace

Heavenly Father,

I come to you today so that I may feel your peace and love. I desperately need you, Lord, to fill me with your Holy Spirit. Help my heart not to feel so troubled or afraid. Do not let my mind be governed by the flesh, but let it be governed by your Holy Spirit that gives life and peace.

In Jesus's name I pray.

Amen.

CHAPTER 16

The Lord Is My Strength

I can do all things through Christ who strengthens me.

—Philippians 4:13 (NKJV)

When our sons were in high school, I helped run the snack bar after school. One day when I was getting ready to do that, our two dogs, Nike and Reebok, decided to bring me a present from the backyard. As I was leaving our bedroom I saw this dead bird on the floor right smack in the middle of the doorway. Our two dogs were looking so happy and proud of the present they brought me.

My reaction was not what the dogs were expecting. I screamed with fear.

The first thing I did was call my husband at work to come home and remove the dead bird. But he was in meetings all day, and I couldn't get ahold of him. So I was left on my own to figure out how to dispose of the bird. I thought maybe I should put a basket over it and have my husband deal with it later. But as I started to do that, I noticed there were mites all over the dead bird. There was no way I could leave it on the floor; I was afraid the dogs would come back for it, since I rejected their present.

Before I go any further, I should mention that I have a huge fear of birds. This was no easy task for me. Time to pray! When I finished praying, a plan for how to dispose of the dead bird began to come together.

I decided to get a trash can and wedge it underneath the bird and flip it up. Yes, that sounded like it would work. "Okay, Lord, I need your help." I began reciting the scripture "I can do all things through Christ who strengthens me" (Philippians 4:13) over and over again as I dragged the trash can in from outside and started wedging it under the dead bird. After several attempts I realized that was not going to work. Another thought came to mind: Get a shovel and put it under the bird, and then flip the bird in the trash can. "Okay," I thought, "that could work." I was still reciting "I can do all things through Christ who strengthens me" as I looked for a shovel.

As I was moving about and calling on God's Word, I could feel God's strength helping me and giving me wisdom and clear direction on how to execute the plan. I once again laid the trash can down as close as possible to the bird. Then I took the shovel with one quick swoop and a screech from me and the bird was in the trash can. Victory!

I picked up the trash can and dragged it and the dead bird outside. Thank you, Lord! I truly can do all things through Christ who strengthens me.

Whether we are trying to do something as simple as getting rid of a dead bird, or dealing with health issues, work issues, or family matters, we need to call on the Lord so he can fill us with his Holy Spirit and his strength. For there is nothing the Lord can't help us get through if we call upon his mighty name.

> Look to the Lord and his strength, seek his
> face always. (1 Chronicles 16:11 NIV)

> Wealth and honor come from you; you are
> the ruler of all things. In your hands are strength
> and power to exalt and give strength to all. (1
> Chronicles 29:12 NIV)

> The LORD is my strength and my shield;
> my heart trusts in him, and he helps me. My

heart leaps for joy, and with my song I praise him. (Psalm 28:7 NIV)

Questions

1) Reread 1 Chronicles 16:11. Where are we to look for strength?

____

____

2) Reread 1 Chronicles 29:12. Who does the Lord give strength to?

____

____

3) Reread Psalm 28:7. What happens when our heart trusts in him?

____

____

4) Reread Philippians 4:13. What can we do when Christ strengthens us?

____

____

5) Think about a time when the Lord provided you with strength and give him praise.

____

____

For Reflection

- We need to look to God.
- We need to pray and ask for God's strength.

- We need to have faith that he will provide us with all we need.
- The Lord is an ever-present help in trouble.

Prayer for Strength

Heavenly Father,

Today I feel weak and so desperately need your strength to get me through this day.

Lord, I look to you and come in prayer asking for you to fill me with your Holy Spirit so that I will be strengthened in you. Provide me with your power, for you, Lord, are my refuge and strength, an ever-present help in trouble.

May I find rest and peace knowing you will provide me with your strength.

In Jesus's name I pray.

Amen.

PART 4

Depending on Prayer

CHAPTER 17

Casting Our Anxiety on the Lord

Do not be anxious about anything, but in every situation, by prayer and petition, with thanksgiving present your requests to God.

—Philippians 4:6 (NIV)

There are times in our lives when we feel anxious. It could be something happening at work, an important decision that has to be made, an upcoming doctor's appointment, or a test you have to take. Any one of these might cause you to lose sleep, to worry, or to find it difficult to concentrate. But this is also the time when you most need to make sure you are praying and petitioning God so that he can renew your mind and replace your thoughts with his perfect peace.

Cast all your anxiety on him [God] because he cares for you. (1 Peter 5:7 NIV)

Questions

1) What makes you feel anxious?

____

____

2)   What can you do to help relieve the anxiety?

____

____

3)   Reread Philippians 4:6. What does God say about being
anxious?

____

____

4)   Reread 1 Peter 5:7. What does Peter tell us to do? Why?

____

____

5)   Think about a time when you were anxious and recall how
you saw God work in the situation.

____

____

For Reflection

- When you start to feel anxious, go to prayer.
- Identify why you are feeling anxious.
- Renew your mind on God's truth.
- Rebuke the enemy and his lies.

Prayers for Casting Our Anxiety on the Lord

Heavenly Father,

I praise your name! Even in the midst of this storm in my life, I praise you! Lord, I ask you to help me navigate through this storm. Give me courage and strength to overcome my fear and weakness. Help me to take captive every anxious thought so that you can replace it with your peace that surpasses all understanding. Help me in my unbelief knowing that you are faithful even when I'm faithless.

Encourage me this day by bringing me hope and help me to continue to praise you!

In Jesus's name I pray.

Amen.

*****

Heavenly Father,

I come before your throne to seek you, Lord, and to seek your ways.

Lord, I come with a heavy heart and need you to help me surrender my thoughts, my ways, and my life to you.

Help me to have a clear understanding of what I am to do. I ask for your wisdom and discernment.

Help me to distinguish what is my part and what is your part. Help me to let go and trust your plan for me, knowing that your plan is perfect.

As I take each step, help me to remember I am not alone and that you are with me.

Fill me with your Holy Spirit, giving me strength and courage to face the tough things in life. And when I begin to get anxious, fearful, or overwhelmed, renew a right spirit in me and fill me with your peace, comfort, and truth so that I can walk in your way for me. Thank you, Lord, that you are with me and you hear my prayers.

In Jesus's name I pray.

Amen.

*****

Heavenly Father,

Here I am, Lord, waiting. And as I'm in this wait mode, I find myself getting anxious and fear is beginning to set in. The "what-ifs" are starting to pop up.

Lord, I ask that you calm my heart and mind. Replace the anxious thoughts and fears with your peace. Help me to remember that you are with me and that you will never leave me and that you are working all things out in your perfect timing.

Lord, you are the God of hope, so help me remain focused on you. For my hope is in you, Lord. Jesus, be near!

In Jesus's name I pray.

Amen.

CHAPTER 18

Battling a Spirit of Fear

For God has not given us a spirit of fear and timidity,
but of power, love, and self-discipline.

—2 Timothy 1:7 (NLT)

From time to time, we all deal with fear of some sort—fear of birds or snakes, flying on planes, being in big water or close spaces, fear of death. And our fears can revolve around a loved one or something we are facing ourselves.

No matter what our fear is, it is real to us, and we need help facing it and overcoming it.

> So do not fear, for I am with you: do not be dismayed for I am your God. I will strengthen you and help you; I will uphold you with my righteous right hand. (Isaiah 41:10 NIV)

Questions

1) What are some fears you are dealing with?

____

____

2)   How do you deal with your fear?

____

____

3)   Do you have an explanation or thoughts of why you have
     these fears?

____

____

4)   Reread 2 Timothy 1:7. What truth does God's Word pro-
     vide that can help you?

____

____

5)   Reread Isaiah 41:10. Why does God say we should not
     fear? What does God say he will do?

____

____

For Reflection

- We need to acknowledge the fear.
- Recognize that this feeling is not of God.
- God did not give us a spirit of fear.
- Ask God to help us work through our fear and give us an
  understanding of why we are fearful.
- Remember God is with us.
- God will strengthen us and help us when we come to him
  in prayer.

Prayers for Battling a Spirit of Fear

Heavenly Father,
     Praise be to the name of God forever and ever!

Your Word says, "So do not fear, for I am with you: do not be dismayed, for I am your God. I will strengthen you and help you; I will uphold you with my righteous right hand" (Isaiah 41:10).

Father God, help me to live each day without fear, trusting that you will strengthen and uphold me no matter what lies before me!

Continue to encourage me today with your Word and your truth.

In Jesus's name I pray.

Amen.

*****

Heavenly Father,

I come before you to lay all my burdens and cares on your mighty throne. Lord, take away the fears and doubts that try to distract me. For your Word says, "For God has not given us a spirit of fear and timidity, but of power, love, and self-discipline" (2 Timothy 1:7 NLT).

Help me to remember your truth when the enemy wants me to believe his lies. May your words ring louder in my ear, in my mind, Lord, and in my heart. Thank you for this day and for your Word.

In Jesus's name I pray.

Amen.

CHAPTER 19

Emptying Yourself of Worry

Who of you by worrying can add a single hour to your life?

—Luke 12:25 (NIV)

One year when our boys were in high school and my stepson had just moved out of our house, I found myself worrying and taking on things that were not mine to carry. That year I passed ten kidney stones just by all the worrying I was doing.

Our youngest son, Christopher, was on a select basketball team that played at different schools in the area. One Sunday, he had a game at a high school that also had a church service going on. So my husband and I dropped our son off at the gym to warm up, and we attended the church service prior to watching his game.

As I sat and listened to the sermon, which was all about worrying, it was as though God was speaking directly to me. He let me know that I was spending way too much time worrying about things I had no control over and which were not really mine to carry.

It took going to this particular service to hear this particular message for me to understand what I needed to be doing.

What I was doing was unhealthy for me. The worrying was like a poison in my body, and I needed to make a change.

God showed me clearly that I only have control over what I do, what I say, and what I think. I have no control over what others do, say, or think. My job is to go to God, lay all those burdens down at his throne, and pray that God would help me to understand my role in each situation and to simply remind me to pray for my children and others to walk in God's will.

> Therefore do not worry about tomorrow, for tomorrow will worry about itself. Each day has enough trouble of its own. (Matthew 6:34 NIV)

Questions

1) What are the things you are worrying about or have worried about?

____

____

2) Do/did you have control over the things you are/were worrying about?

____

____

3) Reread Luke 12:25. What does God's Word say about worrying?

____

____

4) Reread Matthew 6:34. Why does God tell us not to worry about tomorrow?

____

____

5) What steps can you take to not worry?

____

____

For Reflection

- Worrying is unhealthy for you.
- You only have control over what you think and say and do.
- Surrender your worries to God in prayer.
- Ask God for understanding of your role.
- Ask God to help others to walk in his will.

Prayer for Emptying Yourself of Worry

Heavenly Father,

Thank you for your love, your grace, and your mercies that are made new every morning!

Join me this day in all that I do. Help me not to worry about tomorrow but to enjoy what you have for me today. Help me not to fret about what I don't have or what could happen but to focus on and appreciate all that I do have and all that is good in my life. I don't want to miss a thing you have for me! Lord, may I be filled with the fruit of your Holy Spirit—love, joy, peace, patience, kindness, goodness, faithfulness, gentleness, and self-control—and, in some small ways, bring glory to your name.

In Jesus's name I pray.

Amen.

CHAPTER 20

Deciding to Forgive

Make allowance for each other's faults, and forgive
anyone who offends you. Remember, the Lord
forgave you, so you must forgive others.

—Colossians 3:13 (NLT)

There is a time in each of our lives when we will either need to ask for forgiveness or need to forgive someone else. I don't know which is harder: to ask for forgiveness or to forgive. But both are needed.

Some of you right now are saying, "I can't forgive! You don't know what they did to me. If you only knew you wouldn't expect me to forgive them, and God wouldn't ask me to forgive them. It is too hard, and they don't even deserve to be forgiven."

Forgiveness does not mean you forget what they did. It means you choose to obey God and forgive them because God has forgiven you of your offences against him. It means that you no longer allow your anger, bitterness, and resentment to control your life. Instead, you choose to give it to God to handle.

For some, deciding to forgive can take years, for the scars run deep. But please know that the sooner you begin the process of forgiveness, the sooner you can heal from the hurt and pain.

Then Peter came to him and asked, "Lord, how often should I forgive someone who sins against me? Seven times?"

"No, not seven times," Jesus replied, "but seventy times seven!" (Matthew 18:21–22 NLT)

Instead, be kind to each other, tender-hearted, forgiving one another, just as God through Christ has forgiven you. (Ephesians 4:32 NLT)

If you forgive those who sin against you, your heavenly Father will forgive you. But if you refuse to forgive others, your Father will not forgive your sins. (Matthew 6:14–15 NLT)

Questions

1) Reread Colossians 3:13. What does Paul say we should do when others offend us? Why?

____

____

2) Reread Mathew 18:21–22. How many times does Jesus tell Peter we are to forgive someone?

____

____

3) Reread Ephesians 4:32. How does Paul say we should interact with one another?

____

____

4) Think of a time when you needed to ask forgiveness from someone.

____

____

5) Is there someone you need to forgive? Why?

____

____

6) What is stopping you from forgiving? Pray and ask the Lord to help you forgive.

____

____

For Reflection

- Forgiveness is not a feeling; it is a decision.
- To forgive does not mean that what they did was okay.
- To forgive does not mean you forget. It simply means you do not allow the hurt to have power over you anymore. You give it to God to handle.
- We need to forgive fully just as we have been forgiven fully.
- We need to start the process of forgiveness.

Prayer to Forgive Others

Heavenly Father,

I come before you broken and a mess. I come before you with anger, bitterness, resentfulness, and even hate in my heart for the hurt and pain that have been inflicted on me. Lord, you ask me to forgive this person, but in my heart, I don't really want to forgive. But I know you are asking me to be obedient to your Word. Help me, Father, to let go and give it all to you. Help me to make the decision to forgive so that I can begin to heal, not allowing the hurt to have power over my mind, heart, and body.

Help me to forgive fully whether this person ever apologizes or not. I choose to no longer see myself as a victim to the pain and hurt. I will be victorious over it. Help me finally be free. O Lord, give me your strength, your courage, and your heart to forgive.

In Jesus's name I pray.

Amen.

Prayer to Ask for Forgiveness

Heavenly Father,

I come before you ashamed of what I did. I ask, Lord, that you forgive me of the hurt and pain that I have caused and that you would help me to seek forgiveness from those I have hurt.

Father God, help me to be brave and go to those I have wronged. Lord, I ask that you would help them to forgive what I have done and help me to make amends for the hurt and pain that I have caused.

Help me to humbly go before them and ask for forgiveness, not with excuses but with a right spirit and humbled heart.

Lord, I need your strength and your words. I ask that you go with me. Begin to soften their hearts and help them to forgive me. Bring healing to their hearts. Help us to restore what I have broken.

In Jesus's name I pray.

Amen.

Prayer to Forgive Yourself

Heavenly Father,

I struggle with forgiving myself for the poor choices I made in the past.

Lord, I know that as I asked Christ into my life and accepted what he did on the cross, I was forgiven for those past sins. Lord, help me to truly believe that I am redeemed and made clean by Christ's shed blood and sacrifice. Help me let go and not carry these sins any longer.

Help me to believe in my heart that I'm forgiven so that I can be set free and no longer a prisoner to my past sins. Help me, Lord, to rebuke the enemy when he lies to me and says that I am not worthy of your forgiveness.

May I stand firm in your mercy and forgiveness.

In Jesus's name I pray.

Amen.

CHAPTER 21

Feeling Alone

The LORD himself goes before you and will be with
you; he will never leave you nor forsake you.

—Deuteronomy 31:8 (NIV)

The enemy loves to make us feel alone and isolated, thinking that no one cares about us. Holidays and special occasions seem to make us all a little more vulnerable and susceptible to those feelings. When we think of feeling alone, we naturally think of someone who is not in a relationship and has no family. But we can also feel alone even if we are married and have kids. Our spouses may travel a lot. Or when you are together, you're each doing your own thing. When our kids are older and have their own lives and they become busy working and running their kids here and there, once again we can find ourselves vulnerable and feeling forsaken.

God assures us throughout the Old and New Testaments that he will not leave us nor forsake us.

Hold on to God's promise and remember that when we feel alone, we can go to his throne room and know he is waiting for us!

Sometimes, when you feel alone, look around your neighborhood, church, or workplace and maybe extend an invitation to someone else that may not have family or friends nearby and do something together. Or maybe start a group at your church if there isn't one. You will probably find that you are not alone, and others could use the support as well.

If you have a family or have friends that are the same as family, look around and be aware of those that might be alone and hurting and could use an invitation to your table.

> Do not forget to show hospitality to strangers, for by so doing some people have shown hospitality to angels without knowing it. (Hebrews 13:2 NIV)

Questions

1) Are there times in your life that you have felt alone?

____

____

2) How did you overcome those feelings of being alone?

____

____

3) Reread Deuteronomy 31:8. What do you think God wants you to understand through this scripture?

____

____

4) Why might the enemy want you to feel alone?

____

____

5) Reread Hebrews 13:2. What does God say about hospitality?

____

____

For Reflection

- The enemy wants you to feel alone. Do not allow him to win!
- Remember you are never alone, for God is with us always.
- Go to the throne room in prayer.
- Be proactive and look for others that may also feel alone; invite them to your place and start a support/prayer group.

Prayers for Feeling Alone

Heavenly Father,

I thank you that your Word tells us that you will never leave us or forsake us. I pray, Lord, that when the enemy starts to bring thoughts of aloneness or feelings of being forsaken that you will remind me to call out to you for you are with me always. Lord, help me also to have eyes to see others that may be feeling the same way. Give me the courage and strength to speak to them and help us to spur one another on.

Father God, use these feelings to draw me closer to you and others like me so that you may be glorified.

In Jesus's name I pray.

Amen.

*****

Heavenly Father,

I cry out to you, Lord, and ask that you help me to deal with these lonely feelings and thinking no one cares. Father God, I need your help! Jesus, be near! Help me to feel your presence. Help me to focus my mind on your Word, that you love me, that you will never leave me nor forsake me, that I am precious in your sight.

Lord, do not let these lies from the enemy consume me. Do not allow him to rob me of my joy. For you, Lord, came so that I may have life and have life in all its fullness.

In Jesus's name I pray.

Amen.

CHAPTER 22

Looking to the Lord for Healing

Heal me, Lord, and I will be healed; save me and
I will be saved, for you are the one I praise.

—Jeremiah 17:14 (NIV)

It is inevitable that at some point in our lifetime we will have to deal with some kind of health issue.

Some of us will deal with a broken arm or leg. Some will have to have a surgery, but once the surgery is done, we will gradually heal.

Others will have to deal with a disease: diabetes, Crohn's disease, chronic pain, or depression that will never go away, but hopefully can be controlled.

And then there are others that will face life-threatening health issues like cancer or repercussions from a severe accident.

In all cases we need to bring them to the Lord. We need to ask for God's healing over our body and mind. We know that God is the Great Physician. We need not only ask for healing, but believe he will heal us, for we know he is capable. But is he willing?

We are told in 2 Corinthians 12:7–9 that the apostle Paul was given a thorn in his flesh and that he pleaded with the Lord to take it away, but he didn't.

> Therefore, in order to keep me from becoming conceited, I was given a thorn in my flesh, a messenger of Satan, to torment me. Three times I pleaded with the Lord to take it away from me. But he said to me, "My grace is sufficient for you, for my power is made perfect in weakness. Therefore, I will boast all the more gladly about my weakness, so that Christ's power may rest on me." (2 Corinthians 12:7–9 NIV)

We also see in 2 Kings 20 that Hezekiah became ill and at the point of death prayed to the Lord, and he healed him.

> In those days Hezekiah became ill and was at the point of death. The prophet Isaiah son of Amoz went to him and said, "This is what the LORD says: 'Put your house in order, because you are going to die; you will not recover.'" Hezekiah turned his face to the wall and prayed to the LORD. (2 Kings 20:1–2 NIV)

> [Afterward, God said to Isaiah,] "Go back and tell Hezekiah, the leader of my people, 'This is what the LORD, the God of your father David, says: I have heard your prayer and seen your tears; I will heal you.'" (2 Kings 20:5 NIV)

I don't know why God heals some people and not others. I do know what his Word says: "'For my thoughts are not your thoughts, neither are your ways my ways,' declares the LORD. 'As the heavens are higher than the earth, so are my ways higher than your ways and my thoughts than your thoughts'" (Isaiah 55:8–9 NIV).

So, we come before our mighty God in prayer, asking him to heal us, having faith and trusting his plan, understanding that his grace is sufficient and that his power is made perfect in our weakness.

"See now that I myself am he! There is no god besides me. I put to death and I bring to life, I have wounded and I will heal, and no one can deliver out of my hand" (Deuteronomy 32:39 NIV).

"But I will restore you to health and heal your wounds," declares the Lord. (Jeremiah 30:17 NIV)

And he did not do many miracles there because of their lack of faith. (Matthew 13:58 NIV)

He [Jesus] said to her, "Daughter, your faith has healed you. Go in peace and be freed from your suffering." (Mark 5:34 NIV)

Jesus said to him, "Receive your sight; your faith has healed you." (Luke 18:42 NIV)

Is anyone among you sick? Let them call the elders of the church to pray over them and anoint them with oil in the name of the Lord. (James 5:14 NIV)

So Moses cried out to the Lord, "Please, God, heal her!" (Numbers 12:13 NIV)

Questions

1) Reread Deuteronomy 32:39. What is God wanting you to observe from this scripture?

____

____

2) Reread Jeremiah 30:17. Who restores health and heals wounds?

____

____

3) Reread Matthew 13:58. Why was Jesus unable to do many miracles?

____

____

4) Reread Mark 5:34 and Luke 18:42. What helped heal them?

____

____

5) Reread James 5:14 and Numbers 12:13. What is God wanting you to take away from these scriptures? Why do you think it is important?

____

____

For Reflection

- God is the one who brings about life and healing.
- Pray and ask God for healing.
- Have faith he will heal.

- Be open to asking others to intercede and pray for you.
- His grace is sufficient, and his power is made perfect in our weakness.

Prayers for Healing

Heavenly Father,

You are the Great Physician of the world, and I come humbly before you today to ask that you continue to restore me to good health. Heal me, Lord, from the inside out. Strengthen my frame.

Your Word says, "My grace is sufficient for you, for my power is made perfect in weakness" (2 Corinthians 12:9). So I ask that your power be made perfect in me, for I am weak.

In Jesus's name I pray.

Amen.

*****

Heavenly Father,

I need you, Lord. Jesus, be near. Be with me, Lord, as I meet with and talk to the doctors. I ask that you would give the doctors wisdom and discernment in the best way to treat my body. Give me clarity, understanding, and courage as I hear them. I pray that I would walk away encouraged, filled with peace that these are the doctors that can provide the care I need, hopeful that the plan of treatment will free me from this illness. Most importantly, Lord, help me not to feel alone but to remember that you are with me in this battle, fighting for me.

In Jesus's name I pray.

Amen.

*****

Heavenly Father,

I praise you in the middle of the uncertainty of what you are doing in my life. But what I'm certain of is that you are a mighty

God that can heal me, that you are in this battle with me, and that through you I will find the strength and courage I need, so I call upon the mighty name of Jesus to help me.

Give me your grace, for it is sufficient when I am weak, and, Lord, you know that I am weak. Give me peace and a sound mind when it wanders to dark places that are not healthy for me. Help me to take every thought captive and to focus my mind on the things above and not the things on the earth.

Lord, be with me this day!

In Jesus's name I pray.

Amen.

Prayers for Getting Bloodwork Done

Heavenly Father,

As I think about what lies ahead this day, I call on you. I need you to lean on. I need you to help carry me through. I need you to be with me as I enter the building to get my blood work done. I need you to help me as I put my arm out so they can draw my blood. I need you to help me to be calm and not fearful, as I wait for the results. I need you, Lord, to help me have courage and faith no matter what the results reveal. You are with me, and I can face anything and everything that comes my way because I'm leaning on you. You are my Creator, and you are greater and mightier than any friend I could chose to be by my side. Your Word says, "So do not fear, for I am with you; do not be dismayed, for I am your God. I will strengthen you and help you; I will uphold you with my righteous right hand" (Isaiah 41:10).

In Jesus's name I pray.

Amen.

Prayer for Health While I Wait

Heavenly Father,

One of the most difficult things for me to do is wait, Lord. But while I wait, I'm hopeful, even though there is uncertainty all around me. I ask that you help me not to grow faint but stay strong in you,

Lord. Help me to worship you as I wait, trusting that you are working out all the details.

So, God, here I am, Lord! I come to seek you in the midst of my waiting, hopeful that you will do a mighty work in me, healing not only my body, but my mind and heart so that I not only worship you, but I also serve you while I wait upon you. Help me to run this race with confidence and obedience.

I'm trusting you and worshiping you, Lord, while I'm waiting on you!

In Jesus's name I pray.

Amen.

Prayer for Preparing for Surgery

Heavenly Father,

Help me, Lord, to prepare for what lies ahead with my surgery. Give me courage, strength, and healthy mind and heart so that my physical and mental body are ready to undergo surgery.

Help me to get proper sleep and take care of all the details that need to be attended to prior to my surgery so that I'm not worried about unnecessary things.

Help me to remain strong in my faith and in trusting you, Lord. For many times throughout this journey, you have told me to be still, for this battle is yours.

Take away the fears, Lord, and protect my mind and body from the enemy. For you are with me, and your angels will surround me throughout it all.

In Jesus's name I pray.

Amen.

Prayer for the Day of Surgery

Heavenly Father,

I ask that you be with me today. Give me a sense of calmness and peace that all will go smoothly for my surgery.

I trust that you, Lord, will be directing the surgeon's hands and you will equip the medical staff with wisdom, discernment, and a right heart to serve and care for me.

I ask that the surgery will bring healing to my body and that I have a quick and total recovery.

Thank you, Lord, in advance for answered prayers.

In Jesus's name I pray.

Amen.

Prayers for Cancer

Heavenly Father,

In a psalm from King David, his enemies taunt him saying, "'He trusts in the LORD,' they say, 'let the LORD rescue him. Let him deliver him, since he delights in him'" (Psalm 22:8 NIV).

Lord, how I delight in you and trust in you. I ask that you deliver me from this cancer, heal my body, and restore it to good health.

Lord, in the meantime I will worship and praise you, trusting your plan and your timing. I know, Lord, you can deliver me and give me freedom from this cancer. May you be willing.

In Jesus's name I pray.

Amen.

*****

Heavenly Father,

Thank you for all those that are praying for me. I am over-whelmed by their kindness and humbled that so many strangers that don't know me are taking time to pray for me, along with family and friends. Lord, hear their prayers! Give me complete healing over this cancer. Lord, help me to be filled with your spirit. Give me patience as you work all things out to heal me. Help me to be strong in your mighty power. Help me to be courageous in the midst of my fear and uncertainty. Lord, increase my faith. I not only ask, but I believe that you will heal me. Your Word says, "If you have faith as small as a mustard seed, you can say to this mountain, 'Move from here to there,' and it will move. Nothing will be impossible for you" (Matthew 17:20–21).

So, Lord, I ask you to remove this cancer from my body and heal me!

All glory and praise to you!

In Jesus's name I pray.

Amen.

*****

Heavenly Father,

I cry out to you today as my body is still fighting this cancer. Lord, the doctors are all telling me to do different things. I feel frustrated because I don't know how to make the right decision.

So, Lord, I come before your throne, seeking your wisdom, asking you to guide me. I do not know what to do, but my eyes need to be on you. For you, Lord, know my body and you know what the next step is. Help me not to be distracted by all the voices that are speaking to me, but let your voice, Lord, ring louder in my ear than theirs. Help me take the next step that you have ordained for me, trusting and surrendering to your plan for healing me from this cancer.

Lord, as you help me to decipher what to do next, may it bring peace and hope to my heart.

In Jesus's name I pray.

Amen.

*****

Heavenly Father,

This journey has been long and at times has seemed like a death sentence more times than I would like to count. But you, Lord, are using this so that I could see you and draw near to you and understand that I needed to rely on you, not myself.

Only you can raise me and restore my life. Only you are where my hope and my help comes from. This battle is not just mine but yours as well. For you told me repeatedly, I need only be still, for the Lord will fight for me. And repeatedly you have fought and you have delivered me.

Lord, I come before you again asking for you to help me with whatever lies before me. I am setting my hope on you and ask that you once again deliver me, as I need you and am relying on you.

Thank you that my help and my hope is in you, Lord, and that you are faithful.

In Jesus's name I pray.

Amen.

*****

Heavenly Father,

Your Word says: "On him we have set our hope that he will continue to deliver us, as you help us by prayers. Then many will give thanks on our behalf for the gracious favor granted us in answer to the prayers of many" (2 Corinthians 1:10–11).

In you, Father, I put my hope, and I pray that you would continue to deliver me and free me from this cancer. Make my body clean and healthy. Lord, I ask that the pathology report would come back clean and without any signs of cancer.

Lord, I look forward to that day when not only I can give you glory and praise, but the many that have been praying along with me and for me can join me in thanking you and praising you for hearing and answering our prayers.

In Jesus's name I pray.

Amen.

PART 5

Living in Prayer

CHAPTER 23

Praying for Relationships

The LORD God said, "It is not good for the man to
be alone. I will make a helper suitable for him."

—Genesis 2:18 (NIV)

Growing up, one of my favorite things to do was playhouse. I would spend hours playing with my Barbie doll imagining what it would be like to be all grown-up.

For some of you, just like me, you began dreaming at a young age of finding that perfect relationship, our perfect Barbie and Ken. We wanted a relationship that would eventually lead to a "happily-ever-after" marriage, one that lasts a lifetime.

Having had relationships that ended up nowhere, one marriage that didn't last a year, and a second one that is still going strong at thirty-seven years, I can tell you firsthand, relationships and marriage take work. The more you invest in them, by praying and nurturing, guarding your heart, loving and respecting each other, communicating, having fun, and dreaming together, the stronger and the healthier they will be. But the most important thing is to put God in the center of your relationships—especially marriage—continuing to pray and ask God to protect, guide, and bless them.

> Love is patient, love is kind. It does not envy, it does not boast, it is not proud. It is not rude, it is not self-seeking, it is not easily angered, it keeps no record of wrongs. Love does not delight in evil but rejoices with the truth. It always protects, always trusts, always hopes, always perseveres. (1 Corinthians 13:4–7 NIV)

> Above all else, guard your heart for it is the wellspring of life. Put away perversity from your mouth: Keep corrupt talk far from your lips. Let your eyes look straight ahead, fix your gaze directly before you. Make level paths for your feet and take only ways that are firm. Do not swerve to the right or left; Keep your foot from evil. (Proverbs 4:23–27)

> But because of the temptation to sexual immorality, each man should have his own wife and each woman her own husband. (1 Corinthians 7:2 ESV)

> Above all, keep loving one another earnestly, since love covers a multitude of sins. (1 Peter 4:8 ESV)

> For this reason a man will leave his father and mother and be united to his wife, and the two will become one flesh. So they are no longer two, but one flesh. Therefore what God has joined together, let no one separate. (Matthew 19:5–6 NIV)

Questions

1) Reread Genesis 2:18. What does God say about man? What does God say he is going to do?

———————————————————————

———————————————————————

2) How does God describe love in 1 Corinthians 13:4–7?

———————————————————————

———————————————————————

3) Which of the descriptions of love in 1 Corinthians 13:4–7 do you struggle with the most? Why? Which ones are the easiest for you?

———————————————————————

———————————————————————

4) Reread Proverbs 4:23–27. Why does Solomon tell us to guard our hearts above all?

———————————————————————

———————————————————————

5) What things do you need to guard your heart from in your relationship/marriage?

———————————————————————

———————————————————————

6) What steps can you take to guard your heart in your relationship/marriage?

———————————————————————

———————————————————————

7) Reread 1 Corinthians 7:2. Why should each man have his own wife and each woman have her own husband?

———————————————————————

———————————————————————

8) Reread 1 Peter 4:8. What does Peter tell us to do? Why?

____

____

For Reflection

- Invite God into your relationship/marriage.
- Make sure to keep God at the center of your relationship/marriage.
- Pray daily for your relationship/marriage.
- Guard your heart.
- Keep loving one another.
- Love is patient, kind, does not envy, does not boast.
- Love is not proud, it is not rude, is not self-seeking.
- Love is not easily angered, keeps no records of wrongs, and does not delight in evil but rejoices with the truth.
- Love always protects, always trusts, always hopes, and always perseveres.

Prayer for Singles Wanting to Be Married

Heavenly Father,

I look to you, Lord, to help find the husband/wife that you have for me.

In Genesis 2:18, the Lord God said, "It is not good for the man to be alone: I will make a helper suitable for him." Lord, I ask you to bring me a suitable mate, one that lives a godly life and walks in your ways. Give me patience, Lord, to wait for the person you have for me.

Lord, I ask for your will to be done. Whether your plan is for marriage or singleness, help me to be okay with what you have chosen for me. May I trust your plan and make the most of that choice so I can live a life that honors and glorifies you above all.

In Jesus's name I pray.

Amen.

Prayer for Engaged Couples

Heavenly Father,

Thank you for bringing us together, Lord. As we begin to plan our wedding and our life together, help us to remember to invite you to the wedding and to seek your guidance throughout our marriage. May you always remain the center of our lives. Give us wisdom and discernment when we need to make decisions. Help us to guard our hearts at all times so that nothing and no one can separate us from you or our commitment to one another.

Father God, bless this marriage. May our love and commitment last a lifetime, and may we have a marriage that reflects the love of Christ.

In Jesus's name we pray.

Amen.

Prayer for Anniversary

Heavenly Father,

Thank you for this day as we celebrate our marriage. Lord, I ask that you continue to be at the center of our hearts and the center of our marriage.

May each day and each year in our marriage continue to reflect your image. May our love for one another last a lifetime and may we continue to guard our hearts so that we can protect our family. Help us to remain strong in you, Lord, as you journey with us through the good times and the bad.

In Jesus's name I pray.

Amen.

Prayer for Marriage in Need

Heavenly Father,

We need your help, Lord. Jesus, be near. Protect our marriage, Lord. I feel like it is falling apart. Help us to remember our vows and the commitment we made to each other before you. Help us to step back and remember the love that we had for one another and help restore that love now. Help us to understand where we have gone wrong and steer us in the right direction. Help us, Lord, to forgive each other so that we can begin to heal and move forward in renewing our marriage. Do not allow our pride to get in the way. Remove anything or anyone in our lives that does not belong there so that we can honor our commitment and bring restoration to our marriage and family. Heal our marriage, Lord.

In Jesus's name I pray.

Amen.

Prayer for Divorce in Progress

Heavenly Father,

Help us to move forward in a healthy manner from this marriage. Lord, I pray that you would protect our hearts and help us to extend grace and forgiveness where it is needed. Whereas we were once one, we are now torn in two. Bring healing for the hurt and pain. Help our family members to heal as well. In our interactions with one another, may we do so with respect as we learn how to do what is best for our family. Help us to watch over our tongues, our hearts, and our minds so that we can respond in ways that are productive, cooperative, and helpful, enabling healing and preventing destruction to each other and our families.

In Jesus's name I pray.

Amen.

CHAPTER 24

Praying for Children

Children are a gift from the Lord, they are a reward from him.

—Psalm 127:3 (NLT)

Let me begin by saying that children are a gift! Sometimes it may not feel like it when you're up at two in the morning for a feeding or when your teenagers, who were supposed to be home by midnight, are not home at one thirty in the morning, and they're not answering the phones they begged to have.

Every age seems to have its good qualities and challenges. The key is to embrace your precious children right where they are instead of wishing they were past a particular stage. More importantly, pray. Ask God to help you tailor your parenting to the specific needs of each child. Each one was uniquely knitted together by our God and was created for a special work.

> For you created my inmost being, you knit me together in my mother's womb. I praise you because I am fearfully and wonderfully made; your works are wonderful, I know that full well. (Psalm 139:13–14 NIV)

> Before I made you in your mother's womb,
> I chose you. Before you were born, I set you apart
> for a special work. (Jeremiah 1:5 NCV)

We can make plans on what we want our families to be like and how we want to achieve that, but God is ultimately in control.

Throughout our lives, we or others close to us will encounter times of celebration and times of struggles. We will have to make choices that will encourage or challenge our faith. Whatever the situation, we need to be going to the throne room seeking God's guidance, his blessings, his wisdom, and his peace.

> These commandments that I give you today
> are to be upon your hearts. Impress them on your
> children. Talk about them when you sit at home
> and when you walk along the road, when you
> lie down and when you get up. (Deuteronomy
> 6:6–7 NIV)

> Train up a child in the way he should go:
> and even when he is old, he will not depart from
> it. (Proverbs 22:6 NIV)

> I have no greater joy than to hear that my
> children are walking in the truth. (3 John 1:4
> NIV)

> Grandchildren are the crown of the aged,
> and the glory of children is their fathers. (Proverbs
> 17:6 ESV)

Questions

1) Reread Jeremiah 1:5. How does it make you feel knowing that you were chosen before you were in your mother's

womb? Or that your children were chosen before they were in your womb?

____

____

2) How do you feel knowing that even before you were born God set you apart for a special work? How do you feel knowing that your child was set apart for a special work?

____

____

3) What do you think God's special work is for you? For your child?

____

____

4) Reread Deuteronomy 6:6–7. In what ways can you teach your children God's commandments?

____

____

5) Reread Proverbs 22:6. What do you think Solomon means when he says, "Train up a child in the way he should go?"

____

____

For Reflection

- Children are a gift from God.
- We are chosen by God.
- We are set apart for a special work.
- We are to teach our children God's commandments.
- We are to train up children in the way they should go.
- We as parents have no greater joy than hearing that our children are walking in God's truth.

Prayer for the Ability to Have a Child

Heavenly Father,

My heart has a hole in it as I ache and long to have a child. Lord, I cry out like Hannah and ask that you help me to conceive and carry a child to term. I know you are able, God, but are you willing? Help me, Lord, to surrender all to you as you know the plans you have for me. May I have peace no matter what the answer is, trusting your plan is for my good. Help my faith grow stronger and, while I wait, help me continue to worship you.

In Jesus's name I pray.

Amen.

Prayer for Successful Pregnancy

Heavenly Father,

Thank you, Lord, for this precious baby growing inside. We pray that you would continue to help it grow and develop. Keep the baby safe in the womb until it makes its entrance into the world. Lord, we pray that all will go smoothly with labor and delivery of the baby. Give us, as parents, peace, comfort, and strength when needed, helping us to trust your plans, Lord.

Father God, we also ask that you help us to love this baby with the perfect love you would have for it. May we teach our baby all about you and your love so that it will grow up knowing and desiring your ways. May our baby grow up to be a child of God.

In Jesus's name I pray.

Amen.

Prayer for Newborn Child

Heavenly Father,

We thank you for this precious gift of being parents. Lord, we ask that you help us to love this child with a perfect love that is tailored to its specific needs.

Lord, we ask that you help us to teach this child all about you.

May our child have a heart that desires to know you, legs that want to walk in your ways, arms that reach out to others, ears that listen and are attentive to the cares of others, a mouth that praises you and edifies and encourages others, eyes that seek you, Lord, and follow the path you have designed, a nose that can detect when things are wrong, and a mind that is filled with wisdom and discernment. May its body be a temple where your Holy Spirit resides. May this newborn one day be a child of God!

In Jesus's name I pray.

Amen.

Prayer for Grandmothers

Heavenly Father,

Thank you for the gift of being a grandparent. Lord, I'm so excited for this baby to be born. Help me, Lord, to be a woman with sincere faith like Lois, Timothy's grandmother, so I, too, can pass it on to the next generation.

Lord, allow my faith, knowledge, and love for you to be used to encourage each family member to know, love, and worship you, for you are worthy of all our devotion.

In Jesus's name I pray.

Amen.

Prayer for Grandfathers

Heavenly Father,

Thank you for the gift of being a grandfather. Help me to not only love my grandchildren but help me to look for opportunities to share my faith with them. Help my faith be strong and unwavering like Abraham's, and may they not see me but see you, Lord, in me.

Help me, Lord, to appreciate each time I am with my grandchildren, making memories with them that will last a lifetime.

In Jesus's name I pray.

Amen.

Prayer for Giving Up Your Child for Adoption

Heavenly Father,

I need your strength and courage as this is the toughest decision that I have ever had to make.

Lord, my heart is hurting, yet I know giving this baby up for adoption is the right thing to do. I can't provide for its needs.

Lord, may this child never feel rejected by me, but may it know that it is out of deep love and concern that I am doing this.

Lord, find the perfect couple for this baby. May they love this child as their own and care for its every need, keeping it safe and raising it to know you, Lord.

May this child walk in your ways, Lord, and do great things that will bring honor and glory to your name.

In Jesus's name I pray.

Amen.

Prayer for Parents Wanting to Adopt

Heavenly Father,

Our heart cries out for a child, Lord. You have given us this desire in our heart, and I ask that you lead us through the process of adoption.

Lord, we know you have the perfect child for us. Give us direction and next steps to take. Help us trust your plan and your timing. Give us patience and comfort while we go through this long process. Help us not to take our eyes off you and help our faith remain strong.

While we wait, we will worship you, Lord, for you are our hope and are worthy of all our praise.

In Jesus's name I pray.

Amen.

Prayer for Prodigal Children

Heavenly Father,

Our heart is hurting, Lord, over our children's choices. Lord, help us to know how to parent them through this time in their lives.

Help us as parents be like-minded in how to respond and love our children. Lord, you know their hearts and why they are responding in the way they are. Give us your eyes to see them the way you see them. Give us words to speak that will encourage them on the right path. Soften their hearts and open their ears so they can see the destructive choices they are making and want to turn from them. Lord, give them new hearts and minds that want to walk in your ways.

In Jesus's name I pray.

Amen.

Prayer for a Prodigal Child With Addictions

Heavenly Father,

We come before you broken and scared for our children. We pray, Father, that you would take these harmful desires and replace them with a desire for you. Guide us, Lord, and give us wisdom on how to best help our children conquer their addictions. May we, as parents, be like-minded in our responses.

Father, we are so thankful that our children are not alone, but that you are with them. Use this time to draw them close to you. Save our children from this destructive behavior before it takes not only their hearts and minds but their lives.

Lord, help free them from the chains of addiction. Help them not to give into temptation or believe the lies of the enemy, but give them strength and courage to overcome so they may have victory over these addictions once and for all.

Restore them, Lord, with healthy minds and bodies. Give them the desire for you so they may bring glory and honor to you.

In Jesus's name I pray.

Amen.

Prayer for Having Had an Abortion

Heavenly Father,

I come before you ashamed and sorry for the choice I made to have an abortion.

My heart aches for what I have done. Lord, forgive me and cleanse me so that I can begin to heal and move forward.

Lord, restore me to you. Do not let this consume me or separate me from you. Help me to remember that I am redeemed by the blood of Jesus. Thank you, Lord!

In Jesus's name I pray.

Amen.

CHAPTER 25

Praying for Finances

And my God will meet all your needs according
to the riches of his glory in Christ Jesus.

—Philippians 4:19 (NIV)

In the early years of our marriage, we struggled with our finances just like most young couples do. In our first year I became pregnant with our first son. We decided it would be best if I stayed home. Trying to adjust from two incomes to one created challenges. We began to watch our spending. Greg was working hard in sales to provide for us, and I learned to look for sales and clip coupons. It became a game to see how much I could save.

Years went by and Greg began making great money for the family. We lacked for nothing. My husband has a saying, "Money is never a problem as long as you have it." I never really thought about what that meant until we were faced with it again.

Fast-forward to 2008 when the market crashed. We got hit hard. We had two kids in college at the time, so bills were at an all-time high.

I was still not working, only volunteering and leading a women's Bible study. I felt the need to go back to work, but I didn't know what I should do or what I was qualified for as I had been out of the workforce for so long. I began to pray and even told a few friends I was thinking about going back to work, just to get feelers out. Who knew if they might know of something?

As I began praying, God put it on my heart to clean houses. "Clean houses?" I said. "Okay, how do I go about doing that?" That very weekend when my husband and I were at church, I saw one of my friends. She came and sat down beside me. She said, "I don't know if you want it or not, but my mom needs someone to clean her house." Before I knew it I was regularly cleaning houses. The Lord brought me one referral after another. During my daily readings God showed me a scripture: "Humble yourselves, therefore, under God's mighty hand, that he may lift you up in due time" (1 Peter 5:6 NIV).

Six months later, I was given a job opportunity at the church I served and attended.

For three years, I continued to clean houses and work part-time for the church. After the third year, cleaning houses for pay was in the past.

God had provided for our family, helping us to navigate through our financial struggles. Looking back there were lessons for everyone in our family. The most important one was that God provided for our needs as the following scriptures promised!

> If you, then, though you are evil, know how to give good gifts to your children, how much more will your Father in heaven give good gifts to those who ask him! (Matthew 7:11 NIV)

> So do not worry, saying, "What shall we eat?" or "What shall we drink?" or "What shall we wear?" For the pagans run after all these things, and your heavenly Father knows that you need them. But seek first his kingdom and his righteousness, and all these things will be given to you as well. (Matthew 6:31–33 NIV)

> The LORD is my shepherd, I shall not be in want. (Psalm 23:1 NIV)

The lions may grow weak and hungry, but
those who seek the LORD lack no good thing.
(Psalm 34:10 NIV)

Questions

1) Reread Matthew 6:31–33. Do you believe God knows your needs?

____

____

2) What does God mean when he says, "But seek first his kingdom and his righteousness?"

____

____

3) Why do you think God wants you to seek his kingdom first?

____

____

4) Reread Psalm 23:1. What does the psalmist declare?

____

____

5) Reread Psalm 34:10. What does the psalmist say about those who seek the Lord?

____

____

6) Reread Matthew 7:11. Do you believe God wants to give you good gifts?

____

____

7) Looking back on your life, when did you see God provide for you? Pray and give thanks to the Lord.

____

____

For Reflection

- Seek first God's kingdom and his righteousness.
- Pray and ask for God's direction and provisions.
- Believe God will provide.
- God knows your needs.

Prayer for Finances

Heavenly Father,

Lord, I come before you asking for your direction and your provision.

Just as you provided Abraham with a ram as he went to sacrifice Isaac, I ask you to be my Jehovah-Jireh, the Lord that provides.

Please help me to know what I need to do to navigate through this financial situation. Help me not to be fearful or worried, but help me to trust and have faith in you, Lord.

In Jesus's name I pray.

Amen.

Prayer for Needing a Job

Heavenly Father,

I need a job! Please help. You know my skills and you know my passions. I ask that you open doors and show me opportunities for employment. Direct my steps on where to look and give me favor in the interviews. Help me to be confident and bold when you show me where I should work. Lord, lead me and guide me so that I'm in your will for me.

In Jesus's name I pray.

Amen.

PART 6

Practicing to Pray

TURNING SCRIPTURES INTO YOUR PERSONAL PRAYERS

All people are like grass, and all their glory is like the
flowers of the field; the grass withers and the flowers
fall, but the word of the Lord endures forever.

—1 Peter 1:24–25 (NIV)

My life is totally dependent on God's Word. Daily I seek his Word. I wait with great expectations to hear his voice speak to me through my readings. Some days I'm just reading to know him more, and other days it is as though he illuminates a verse just when I need him the most. His Word has been and is life-changing to me and can be for you as well.

In this chapter you will find scriptures on several topics that I have turned into personal prayers. You can use these prayers as a guide when you don't know what to pray for or how to pray. Or you can create your own prayers using these scriptures and others that are pertinent to your situation.

My hope is that the Lord will touch your heart and give you a hunger for his Word and that your ears will be attentive to the times he speaks to you through his Word.

Anxiety

> Anxiety weighs down the heart, but a kind
> word cheers it up. (Proverbs 12:25 NIV)

> Cast all your anxiety on him because he cares for you. (1 Peter 5:7 NIV)

Heavenly Father,

I come with a heavy heart full of anxiety. Lord, help me to let go and give my cares to you instead of holding onto them and allowing them to consume me.

Lord, help me to remember I can come to you about anything and everything. Because nothing is too small or too big for you to handle, I am confident that you will work things out. Thank you for the way you love and care for me.

In Jesus's name I pray.

Amen.

Faith

> If you do not stand firm in your faith, you will not stand at all. (Isaiah 7:9 NIV)

> "Have faith in God," Jesus answered. "Truly I tell you, if anyone says to this mountain, 'Go, throw yourself into the sea,' and does not doubt in their heart but believes that what they say will happen, it will be done for them. Therefore I tell you, whatever you ask for in prayer, believe that you have received it, and it will be yours." (Mark 11:22–24 NIV)

> He replied, "If you have faith as small as a mustard seed, you can say to this mulberry tree, 'Be uprooted and planted in the sea,' and it will obey you." (Luke 17:6 NIV)

> Therefore, since we have been justified through faith, we have peace with God through our Lord Jesus Christ, through whom we have

gained access by faith into this grace in which we now stand. (Romans 5:1–2 NIV)

And without faith it is impossible to please God, because anyone who comes to him must believe that he exists and that he rewards those who earnestly seek him. (Hebrews 11:6 NIV)

Heavenly Father,

I believe that you exist, and I come earnestly to seek you! Lord, as I draw near to you today, I ask that you continue to reveal yourself to me. Help me to understand your Word, recognize your voice, and feel your presence even though I don't see you. Help me not to doubt. Lord, increase my faith so that it will be pleasing to you.

In Jesus's name I pray.

Amen.

Fear

Even though I walk through the darkest valley, I will fear no evil, for you are with me; your rod and you staff, they comfort me. (Psalm 23:4 NIV)

I sought the LORD, and he answered me: he delivered me from all my fears. (Psalm 34:4 NIV)

Therefore we will not fear, though the earth give way and the mountains fall into the heart of the sea. (Psalm 46:2 NIV)

Fear of man will prove to be a snare, but whoever trusts in the LORD is kept safe. (Proverbs 29:25 NIV)

> Say to those with fearful hearts, "Be strong, do not fear; your God will come, he will come with vengeance, with divine retribution he will come to save you." (Isaiah 35:4 NIV)

> So do not fear, for I am with you; do not be dismayed, for I am your God. I will strengthen you and help you; I will uphold you with my righteous right hand. (Isaiah 41:10 NIV)

> For I am the LORD your God who takes hold of your right hand and says to you, "Do not fear; I will help you." (Isaiah 41:13 NIV)

> For God has not given us a spirit of fear and timidity, but of power, love, and self-discipline. (2 Timothy 1:7 NLT)

Heavenly Father,

The enemy is near and is trying to consume me with fear, anxiety, and worry. So I run to you, Lord, this morning and ask you to replace those thoughts and feelings with your peace, comfort, and strength.

Help me to remember your Word in 2 Timothy 1:7, "For God has not given us a spirit of fear and timidity but of power, love and self-discipline."

Fill me with your power, Lord, to overcome the enemy. Help me trust in your love for me, and help me to discipline myself as I wait for your direction.

In Jesus's name I pray.

Amen.

Finances

> The LORD is my Shepherd, I shall not be in want. (Psalm 23:1 NIV)

The lions may grow weak and hungry, but those who seek the Lord lack no good thing. (Psalm 34:10 NIV)

So do not worry, saying, "What shall we eat?" or "What shall we drink?" or "What shall we wear?" For the pagans run after all these things, and your heavenly Father knows that you need them. But seek first his kingdom and his righteousness, and all these things will be given to you as well. (Matthew 6:31–33 NIV)

If you, then, though you are evil, know how to give good gifts to your children, how much more will your Father in heaven give good gifts to those who ask him! (Matthew 7:11 NIV)

And my God will meet all your needs according to the riches of his glory in Christ Jesus. (Philippians 4:19 NIV)

Heavenly Father,

I praise your holy name, for you are my rock, my strength, and my provider.

I come before you trusting your Word in Philippians 4:19 that says you will meet all my needs according to the riches of your glory in Christ Jesus.

Father God, you know all my needs and I ask for your provisions. Help me not to doubt but trust in your Word. Show me what my part is and what I need to do.

Thank you in advance for being my Jehovah-Jireh: the Lord that provides.

In Jesus's name I pray.

Amen.

Forgiveness

> If you forgive those who sin against you, your heavenly Father will forgive you. But if you refuse to forgive others, your Father will not forgive your sins. (Matthew 6:14–15 NLT)

> Then Peter came to him and asked, "Lord, how often should I forgive someone who sins against me? Seven times?"
> "No, not seven times," Jesus replied, "but seventy times seven!" (Matthew 18:21–22 NLT)

> Instead be kind to each other, tenderhearted, forgiving one another, just as God through Christ has forgiven you. (Ephesians 4:32 NLT)

> Make allowance for each other's faults, and forgive anyone who offends you. Remember, the Lord forgave you, so you must forgive others. (Colossians 3:13 NLT)

Heavenly Father,

You tell me in Colossians 3:13 that I need to forgive anyone who offends me. Lord, I am having a hard time doing that. But I want to be obedient to your Word, which also says, "Remember, the Lord forgave you, so you must forgive others" (Colossians 3:13). Lord, soften my heart and help me to make allowances for their faults just as you have made allowances for mine. Help me to let go of the bitterness, anger, and hurt so that I no longer carry this burden around with me. But help me to surrender it to you so that I may live my life in obedience to your Word and your will for me. Heal my heart, Lord, and make it whole again.

In Jesus's name I pray.

Amen.

Healing and Health

So Moses cried out to the LORD, "Please, God, heal her!" (Numbers 12:13 NIV)

See now that I myself am he! There is no god besides me. I put to death and I bring to life, I have wounded and I will heal, and no one can deliver out of my hand. (Deuteronomy 32:39 NIV)

Then the king said to the man of God, "Intercede with the LORD your God and pray for me that my hand may be restored." So the man of God interceded with the Lord, and the king's hand was restored and became as it was before. (1 Kings 13:6 NIV)

Who forgives all your sins and heals all your diseases. (Psalm 103:3 NIV)

"But I will restore you to health and heal your wounds," declares the LORD. (Jeremiah 30:17 NIV)

And he did not do many miracles there because of their lack of faith. (Matthew 13:58 NIV)

He said to her, "Daughter, your faith has healed you. Go in peace and be freed from your suffering." (Mark 5:34 NIV)

Jesus said to him, "Receive your sight; your faith has healed you." (Luke 18:42 NIV)

Is anyone among you sick? Let them call the elders of the church to pray over them and anoint them with oil in the name of the Lord. (James 5:14 NIV)

Heavenly Father,

I come to you, Lord, to ask for healing in my body. You instruct us in James 5:14 to call on the elders of the church to pray over us when we are sick. Lord, as I call on them, may they be willing to pray over me and anoint me with oil in the name of the Lord. Provide them with your power, and as they pray, Lord, may you hear their prayers and be willing to heal me and restore me to good health.

In Jesus's name I pray.

Amen.

Hope

We put our hope in the LORD. He is our help and our shield. In him our hearts rejoice, for we trust in his holy name. Let your unfailing love surround us, LORD, for our hope is in you alone. (Psalm 33:20–22 NLT)

May those who fear you rejoice when they see me, for I have put my hope in your word. (Psalm 119:74 NIV)

I wait for the LORD, my soul waits, and in his word I put my hope. (Psalm 130:5 NIV)

The LORD delights in those who fear him, who put their hope in his unfailing love. (Psalm 147:11 NIV)

But those who hope in the LORD will renew their strength. They will soar on wings like eagles; they will run and not grow weary; they will walk and not be faint. (Isaiah 40:31 NIV)

"For I know the plans I have for you," declares the LORD, "plans to prosper you and not to harm you, plans to give you hope and a future." (Jeremiah 29:11 NIV)

May the God of hope fill you with all joy and peace as you trust in him, so that you may overflow with hope by the power of the Holy Spirit. (Romans 15:13–15 NIV)

Heavenly Father,

You are the King of kings, Lord of lords, and God of all gods. You are the God of hope.

Lord, I ask that you give me strength to deal with my troubles and help me to overcome these feelings of fear and worry. Replace them all with your joy and peace as I seek you and trust in you. May I overflow with hope by the power of your Holy Spirit.

In Jesus's name I pray.

Amen.

Marriage

For this reason a man will leave his father and mother and be united to his wife, and the two will become one flesh. So they are no longer two, but one flesh. Therefore, what God has joined together, let man not separate. (Matthew 19:5–6 NIV)

Husbands, love your wives, just as Christ loved the Church and gave himself up for her. (Ephesians 5:25 NIV)

However, each of you also must love his wife as he loves himself and the wife must respect her husband. (Ephesians 5:33 NIV)

Heavenly Father,
I will praise you among the people. For great is your love!
Lord, I ask that you would help us to honor you in our marriage.
Help us to live out our days as you would have us do: a husband that loves his wife like he loves himself and a wife that respects her husband. Remind us to live each day committed to you, Lord, and to each other. May our marriage reflect your image so others may see and give glory to you.
In Jesus's name I pray.
Amen.

Peace

The LORD gives strength to his people; the Lord blesses his people with peace. (Psalm 29:11 NIV)

Peace I leave with you, my peace I give you. I do not give to you as the world gives. Do not let your hearts be troubled and do not be afraid. (John 14:27 NIV)

I have told you these things, so that in me you may have peace. In this world you will have trouble. But take heart! I have overcome the world. (John 16:33 NIV)

The mind governed by the flesh is death, but the mind governed by the Spirit is life and peace. (Romans 8:6 NIV)

> For God is not a God of disorder but of peace—as in all the congregations of the Lord's people. (1 Corinthians 14:33 NIV)

> Do not be anxious about anything, but in every situation by prayer and petition, with thanksgiving, present your requests to God. And the peace of God, which transcends all understanding, will guard your hearts and your minds in Christ Jesus. (Philippians 4:6–7 NIV)

Heavenly Father,

My mind and heart are out of control with thoughts and feelings that are not of you.

As instructed in Philippians 4:6, I come asking you to help me take captive every thought that is not of you. I long for your peace that transcends all understanding because I know that peace will guard my heart and mind in Christ Jesus and enable me to be filled afresh with your Holy Spirit.

In Jesus's name I pray.

Amen.

Strength

> Look to the Lord and his strength; seek his face always. (1 Chronicles 16:11 NIV)

> Wealth and honor come from you; you are the ruler of all things. In your hands are strength and power to exalt and give strength to all. (1 Chronicles 29:12 NIV)

> The LORD is my strength and my shield; my heart trusts in him, and he helps me. My heart leaps for joy, and with my song I praise him. (Psalm 28:7 NIV)

> God is our refuge and strength, an ever-present help in trouble. (Psalm 46:1 NIV)

> The LORD is my strength and my defense, he has become my salvation. (Psalm 118:14 NIV)

> I can do all things through Christ who strengthens me. (Philippians 4:13 NKJV)

Heavenly Father,

I am overwhelmed with all that is going on in my life. My heart is heavy, and my mind and body feel weak.

I come before your holy throne, Lord, to proclaim your Word in Philippians 4:13, "I can do all things through Christ who strengthens me."

Lord, strengthen me physically and mentally. Provide me with your strength so that I can accomplish what needs to be done. Help me to trust that I can do all things that are before me because you are with me, empowering me through your Holy Spirit.

In Jesus's name I pray.

Amen.

Trust

> But I trust in your unfailing love. I will rejoice because you have rescued me. (Psalm 13:5 NLT)

> But when I am afraid, I will put my trust in you. (Psalm 56:3 NLT)

> Those who trust in the LORD are like Mount Zion, which cannot be shaken but endures forever. (Psalm 125:1 NIV)

> Trust in the Lord with all your heart and lean not on your own understanding; in all your ways submit to him, and he will make your paths straight. (Proverbs 3:5–6 NIV)

> Trust in the LORD forever, because GOD the LORD is the Rock eternal. (Isaiah 26:4 BSB)

> The LORD is good, a refuge in times of trouble. He cares for those who trust in him. (Nahum 1:7 NIV)

Heavenly Father,

Lord, I praise your holy name for you are good.

I come to your throne and cry out to you, Lord, as trouble surrounds me. I need you, Lord, to be my refuge. I trust you to lead me and guide my steps. Provide me with the courage and strength that I need to carry out my part so I may be delivered from all my troubles.

Lord, I'm so thankful that you care for me, for your Word tells us you care for those who trust in you.

In Jesus's name I pray.

Amen.

Worry

> Therefore I tell you, do not worry about your life, what you will eat or drink; or about your body, what you will wear. Is not life more than food, and the body more that clothes? (Matthew 6:25 NIV)

> Who of you by worrying can add a single hour to your life? (Luke 12:25 NIV)

Heavenly Father,

My mind and heart are consumed with worry.

Lord, I ask that you help me to take every thought captive and to focus my mind on things above, instead of the "what-ifs."

Help me to understand what I can control and not to worry, but pray, about what I can't control.

Remind me that worry is like a poison to my body. Help me to recall your words from Luke 12:25, "Who of you by worrying can add a single hour to your life?"

Lord, replace the worry and fill me with your spirit of peace.

In Jesus's name I pray.

Amen.

AN IMPORTANT REMINDER

No matter what the day before brought—hurt, pain, frustration, anxiety, or fear—today is a new day with new beginnings. And each day provides us with new opportunities to pray and see God work, if only we would remember to stop and pray. Pray about everything!

Come to the holy throne of God and ask him to help you be the person he created you to be. On our own we struggle, but with God, all things are possible!

> Forget the former things; do not dwell on the past. See, I am doing a new thing! Now it springs up; do you not perceive it. (Isaiah 43:18–19 NIV)

> With God, all things are possible. (Matthew 19:26 NIV)

Always stop and pray (ASAP).

ACKNOWLEDGMENTS

I have to start out by thanking our awesome God, for he is the one that inspired and surrounded me with the people that could help make this book possible. To him be all the glory!

I want to thank my superhero husband, Greg. From the first moment I mentioned God laid on my heart to write a prayer book, he supported, encouraged, and even said, "I'll help by taking all your handwritten rough drafts and type them up for you." Revision after revision, moving chapters around, being my sounding board, to saying, "Whatever it takes, we will get your book published," you are the one that never doubted but believed in me, and it meant so much.

A huge thank-you to my dear friend and sister in Christ Dixie Richards for agreeing to help edit my book. You helped me so much! Getting me organized, editing my writing, challenging me, and all your time and patience are so appreciated. You helped me make what God laid on my heart a reality! I can never thank you enough!

To my son Roy and my daughter-in-law Halie, thank you! I can still remember both of your encouragement and enthusiasm as I told you God was having me write a prayer book. Roy, you had tons of suggestions and even began making calls and texting people that very day on how to get started. You even created a mock book cover that gave me encouragement and a glance that this book could be a reality. Halie, your prayers and encouraging words touched my heart and helped me believe and see that this book has something to offer others.

Thank you to my son Christopher for his support and allowing me to share part of his life's journey with cancer. The battle truly was the Lord's, and the victory and praise all goes to God.

To my dear friend Leslie Bolling, thank you for being my number one cheerleader! Your encouragement along this journey of writing this book inspired me to keep going. You were the first person to read my manuscript other than my husband and Dixie. I loved how you kept sending me texts updating me on where you were in reading the book. You kept saying how you loved the book. I remember how that made me feel, full of tears and happiness, as you validated what God had asked me to do.

To my wonderful friend Sue Moye, thank you for always being honest, challenging me and inspiring me throughout this journey. I so valued your feedback on my manuscript. I remember when I first told you I was going to write a prayer book, you said to me, "Oh, Terri, I'm so excited for you. All your times you prayed with others and brought them to the throne room, and now you can help others to experience it as well." Those words meant so much, for you are someone I have always looked up to.

Pastor Cindy Grasso, thank you so much for taking the time to read my manuscript and giving me your feedback full of encouragement.

Thank you to Shannon, Lisa, and all the others at Christian Faith Publishing for helping me to publish *On My Knees*.

To our couples' small group, my Suitland Sisters, and to the many others who prayed for me as I wrote this book, thank you!